COMBAT AIRCRAFT SERIES

A-4 Skyhawk

LINDSAY PEACOCK

OSPREY PUBLISHING LONDON

Published in 1987 by
Osprey Publishing Ltd
Member Company of the George Philip Group
27a Floral Street, London WC2E 9DP

British Library Cataloguing in Publication Data

Peacock, Lindsay T.
    A-4 Skyhawk—(Osprey combat aircraft).
    1. Skyhawk bomber
    I. Title
    623.7′63   UG1242.B6

ISBN 0-85045-817-X

Typeset by Flair plan Photo-typesetting Ltd.
Printed in Hong Kong

Colour artworks © Pilot Press Ltd, Mike Keep
and © Bedford Editions Ltd.
Cutaway drawing: Pilot Press Ltd.
Photographs: Supplied by McDonnell Douglas Corporation,
the US Department of Defense and Richard Leask Ward.

The Author
LINDSAY PEACOCK is an aviation journalist and
photographer who has written extensively on military
aircraft subjects for books and magazines, especially in
areas of specific interest to aircraft modellers. He has
travelled widely in pursuit of his profession and hobbies,
and spent much time at military aircraft establishments
observing his subjects at close quarters. His other books in
this series are F/A-18 Hornet, F-14 Tomcat, B-52
Stratofortress, AH-1 HueyCobra, and A-4 Skyhawk.

Contents

1
Design and Development

ANY DETAILED study of the post-war military aviation scene in the USA will quickly reveal that the 1950s was indeed a special decade, the various manufacturers conceiving and producing an almost bewildering succession of warplanes. Today, of course, few of the types which made their debuts then are still to be found in the USA's impressive arsenal. Nevertheless, there are two types which might now be said to occupy a position of "elder statesman" for both have recently embarked upon their fourth decade of front-line service.

Boeing's B-52 Stratofortress is one, this massive eight-engined bomber still featuring prominently in Strategic Air Command's war plans some 32 years after the first examples were delivered. In contrast, the second survivor of that era lies at the other end of the weight scale, in the shape of the diminutive Douglas A-4 Skyhawk.

In its initial form as the A4D-1 (later redesignated A-4A), this was a true lightweight, tipping the scales at a modest 8,400lb (3,812kg) when empty whereas early production B-52s in similar configuration weighed around 175,000lb (79,401kg). When it

came to gross weight, the difference was even more marked, corresponding figures being 20,000lb (9,074kg) and 420,000lb (190,563kg). Little wonder that the Skyhawk quickly acquired the nicknames "Scooter" and "Tinker Toy Bomber"; these apparently disparaging epithets were actually terms of endearment, for the A-4 went on to demonstrate that it possessed a remarkable ability to absorb punishment which might well have caused the destruction of other less robust aircraft.

Rugged construction proved advantageous in other ways. A two-seat derivative was selected to serve as the Navy's advanced jet trainer and succeeding generations of jet combat pilots have earned their "wings" on the TA-4J since 1970. In addition, single and two-seat Skyhawks also proved suitable for the fighter adversary role, initially with the Navy's Fighter Weapons School ("Top Gun") at Miramar, California and eventually with a number of "aggressor" squadrons such as VF-43 at Oceana.

Going back in time, Skyhawk evolution effectively

Below: with the designation and bureau number obscured, the prototype Douglas XA4D-1 Skyhawk made its debut in a basically silver finish relieved only by national insignia and Navy titles.

Above: Carrying auxiliary fuel tanks on each of the three stores stations, Bu.No. 142191 is a late production A4D-1 Skyhawk and wears the standard gull grey and white finish of the late 1950s.

arose out of a requirement to replace an earlier attack aircraft from the Douglas stable, namely the AD (later A-1) Skyraider. Initial studies were based on the Navy's request for a twin-turboprop aircraft capable of delivering a 2,000lb (907kg) payload and possessing a combat radius of some 460 miles (736km). The Douglas response to this was the XA2D-1 Skyshark which was powered by an Allison T40 engine driving contra-rotating propellers. As it turned out, the Skyshark was doomed to failure, largely as a result of engine-related problems. But, even as Skyshark testing was under way, the chief engineer at Douglas Aircraft's El Segundo, California factory was hard at work on a very different concept. It was this which led to the Skyhawk.

Ed Heinemann was the engineer concerned and the Skyhawk was very much a one-man show during the early stages, the design arising from a series of studies into a lightweight fighter interceptor in the 8,000lb (3,628kg) class. This study was used as the basis of a presentation on aircraft growth factors given by Heinemann to senior Navy officers in Washington in January 1952. One of those present was Rear Admiral Apollo Soucek, who was evidently sufficiently impressed by Heinemann's arguments to enquire if the data could be applied to an attack aircraft.

Heinemann's response was positive and affirmative, the upshot being that he was requested to prepare a definite proposal. Little more than a month later, he was back in Washington where his concept was received somewhat cautiously. This caution almost certainly arose from the fact that Heinemann's proposal had a gross weight less than half that originally stipulated by the Bureau of Aeronautics (BuAer) when it first started looking for a

Below: With no fewer than 542 examples built, the A4D-2 was the second most numerous Skyhawk derivative and was also the first version to feature provision of in-flight refuelling capability.

Skyraider replacement.

Nevertheless, the Navy was sufficiently impressed to award Douglas a contract for an initial batch of 20 aircraft. Placed in June 1952, this was primarily for pre-production prototypes.

Barely two years elapsed between placement of this contract and the maiden flight, the latter event taking place on 22 June 1954 when Douglas test pilot Robert Rahn took the XA4D-1 prototype (Bu.No.137812) aloft from Edwards AFB, California. There then followed two years of intense development flying, highlights occurring in September 1955 when the Skyhawk earned its sea legs aboard the USS *Ticonderoga* and on 15 October 1955 when an A4D-1 (Bu.No.137814) piloted by Lt Gordon Gray established a new world speed record over a 500-km (310.7 mile) closed circuit course at Edwards, flashing round at low level at 695.127mph (1,112.2km/h). In the process, it became the first attack aircraft to hold such a record.

First contracts

By then, the Navy had acknowledged the Skyhawk's undoubted promise in the best way possible by placing the first of a long series of production contracts. This covered 52 A4D-1s (Bu.Nos.139919-139970) and delivery to the fleet began on 9 September 1956 when VA-72 accepted its initial example at Quonset Point NAS, Rhode Island. Subsequently, a further 94 A4D-1s (Bu.Nos.142142-142235) were completed before production switched to the A4D-2 (later A-4B) model.

By today's standards, the work-up to operational status was amazingly quick, for VA-72 was declared operational on 26 October, less than seven weeks

Above: Seen being muscled into position for launch, this A-4C is from VA-95, one of three Skyhawk-equipped squadrons aboard the USS *John F. Kennedy* for that carrier's 1969 Mediterranean cruise.

after receiving its first aircraft. Admittedly, in its original guise, the Skyhawk was fairly unsophisticated but even allowing for that the pace of the ensuing re-equipment programme was impressive. A second Atlantic Fleet squadron (VA-34) had begun conversion by the end of the same year while deliveries to the Pacific Fleet had also got under way, VA-93 at Alameda becoming the first West Coast-based unit.

Then, in January 1957, the Marine Corps also got its hands on the Skyhawk when VMA-224 at El Toro began conversion, this unit also picking up A4D-1s. By the end of 1957, six more Navy squadrons and another USMC unit had followed suit, the latter (VMA-211) being first to utilise the improved A4D-2 in September 1957.

Eventually, no fewer than 51 front-line Navy and Marine Corps squadrons operated variations on the Skyhawk theme, making it quite definitely one of the most successful post-war US combat aircraft. A small irony of the Skyhawk saga was the fact that it never actually evolved into a replacement for the A-1 "Spad"—as had been the original intention.

Instead, it supplanted other jet types such as the F9F-8 Cougar and FJ-4 Fury in the light attack role, in the process serving beside the Skyraider which fulfilled the medium attack mission. Indeed, Douglas enjoyed a state of monopoly for several years when it came to providing the Navy with attack aircraft since this company was also responsible for the A3D Skywarrior which equipped heavy attack squadrons.

The desire to save unnecessary weight was one of

the key criteria in the design of the Skyhawk, and it followed more or less automatically that the finished product would be relatively unsophisticated. Nonetheless, despite the fact that simplicity was inherent in the Skyhawk concept, it would be incorrect to say that it failed to break new ground. For example it marked a welcome reversion of the trend towards ever more heavy and complex warplanes. This, in turn, meant that often imaginative solutions were necessary to overcome "problem" areas, a good example of these being provided by the landing gear, which lacked an emergency hydraulic system. In the event of failure of the prime system, all three oleo legs were designed to respond to Newton's law, emergency extension being accomplished by a mix of good old-fashioned gravity and aerodynamic pressure. A simple but highly effective solution, this epitomised the approach that was adopted throughout.

As far as the basic structure is concerned, confirmation that the Douglas engineers got it pretty much right first time is provided by the fact that the Skyhawk changed only slightly during a production run which spanned more than 25 years. Inevitably, there were instances of "add-ons"—the dorsal avionics pack introduced on the A-4F and later retrofitted to many A-4Es and remanufactured A-

4Cs being perhaps the most visible—but, by and large, the last A-4Ms retained a striking resemblance to those produced more than 20 years earlier. Beneath the skin, of course, it was another matter entirely. The avionics "fit" was subjected to continuous refinement throughout the course of production with the result that the A-4M was a vast improvement over the original A-4A.

To return to the structure, the airframe comprised just three major assemblies—wing, forward fuselage and aft fuselage with the latter incorporating horizontal and vertical tail surfaces. Each of these assemblies was manufactured separately, with the various items of internal equipment, control runs and associated electrical systems being installed before mating.

All-metal semi-monocoque construction was employed for front and rear fuselage sections, the forward portion employing a detachable nose cone over the fully integrated avionics pack, including navigation, IFF and communications equipment, which was mounted on the forward fuselage bulkhead. On the later model A-4s, which embodied a more complex avionics suite, the dorsal area was dominated by a bulbous fairing which many felt spoilt the Skyhawk's lines.

Maximising pilot efficiency was the name of the game when it came to cockpit design, this being somewhat utilitarian, at least on early models. Wherever possible, instruments were combined while those items which were considered as "lux-

Below: Probably taken in the late 1950s, these two A4D-2s are from different USMC squadrons, that in the foreground being assigned to VMA-332 While the rear machine is from H&MS-12.

uries" were deleted altogether in deference to weight reduction. An ejection seat was provided but Douglas opted to use its own Escapac seat which offered a weight saving of around 60 per cent when compared with the standard Navy article.

Directly aft of the cockpit was a 240 US gallon (9081) fuel tank and behind that lay the engine, air for this being furnished by intakes mounted high on the fuselage sides. On early production Skyhawks, Wright's J65 was fitted as standard, this licence-built copy of the Armstrong-Siddeley Sapphire giving way to the Pratt & Whitney J52 with effect from the A-4E.

Three frames

The aft fuselage section was built up around three major frames, one of which was connected to the rear wing spar while another bore arrester hook loadings. The third was connected to the fin spar and also carried the variable incidence tailplane pivot connections. Front and rear fuselage attachment occurred at the intermediate wing spar and required just six bolts, and it was possible to remove the entire aft section on a special dolly, making the task of changing an engine relatively simple. In addition to vertical and horizontal tail surfaces, the aft fuselage also featured a pair of hydraulically-actuated speed brakes, these hinging out from the lower fuselage sides.

The wing was manufactured as a single assembly

Above: Testing the effectiveness of fire from three Hipeg gun pods, Bu.No. 145063 was the second A-4C built and spent virtually all of its flying career with the Naval Weapons Center at China Lake.

and essentially consisted of a three-spar box with the spars being machined from the solid. Serving as an integral fuel tank with a capacity of 560 US gal (2,1201), wing-to-fuselage attachment was effected by 10 steel bolts, these connecting to major frames at the leading edge, front, intermediate and rear spars and trailing edge channel section.

The Skyhawk's short span wing eliminated the need for weighty wing-fold mechanisms although it should be noted that at least one A-4A acquired wing and vertical tail folding capability. Quite why this was done remains unclear but it may well have been

Below: The second of two A4D-5 prototypes is seen in flight with a full bag of conventional iron bombs on the centreline and inner wing hardpoints plus Bullpup missiles on the outer weapons rails.

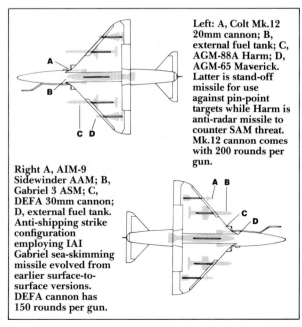

Left: A, Colt Mk.12 20mm cannon; B, external fuel tank; C, AGM-88A Harm; D, AGM-65 Maverick. Latter is stand-off missile for use against pin-point targets while Harm is anti-radar missile to counter SAM threat. Mk.12 cannon comes with 200 rounds per gun.

Right A, AIM-9 Sidewinder AAM; B, Gabriel 3 ASM; C, DEFA 30mm cannon; D, external fuel tank. Anti-shipping strike configuration employing IAI Gabriel sea-skimming missile evolved from earlier surface-to-surface versions. DEFA cannon has 150 rounds per gun.

intended to facilitate transport by road, the aircraft concerned possibly being employed as an aid to recruitment. Certainly, there appears to be little evidence to support the belief that it ever flew in this configuration.

Control surfaces were nothing if not conventional, comprising trailing edge flaps, ailerons, all-flying horizontal tail and a rudder. The rudder was subject to change at an early stage, the original being found to generate unacceptable "buzz". With effect from the A-4B the so-called "tadpole" rudder was adopted, this employing a single skin with external reinforcing ribs on either side. Thereafter, all Skyhawks shared this distinctive feature. In addition, automatic leading edge slats were fitted as standard.

Turning to weaponry, the A4D-1 featured a pair of Colt Mk.12 20-mm cannon, one buried in each wing root. This gun was an ever present feature of succeeding single-seat Skyhawks for the Navy and Marines as well as the two-seat TA-4F. Ammunition was contained in rotating drums designed to facilitate feeding and minimise jamming problems but capacity was perhaps not all it might have been, only 100 shells being provided for each gun. Eventually, on the A-4M, capacity was increased to 200 rounds per gun. Some export models, such as the A-4H/N, employ a different gun system.

On the early production models, three external stores stations were also provided, one on the centreline and one under each wing. These were able to carry a variety of ordnance, including "special" (i.e. nuclear) weapons, conventional "iron" bombs, Bullpup missiles, unguided Zuni rocket pods and napalm. With effect from the A-4E, the number of pylons was increased to five and ordnance options

have also expanded to include newer generations of bomb as well as "smart" weapons such as the AGM-65 Maverick and air-to-air missiles like the AIM-9 Sidewinder. On the ultimate A-4M version, capacities were 3,500lb (1,588kg) on the centreline station; 2,250lb (1,021kg) on the inboard wing stations and 1,000lb (454kg) on the outboard wing stations, giving a theoretical maximum payload of 10,000lb (4,538kg). In practice, the aircraft would be unlikely to operate with anything like this load.

Auxiliary fuel tanks may be carried by three of the external stores stations, the inner wing and centreline points all being "plumbed" for fuel transfer. A maximum of 1,000 US gal (3,786l) of fuel may be carried in this way, augmenting the A-4M's internal fuel capacity of 800 US gal (3,028l) and bestowing a maximum ferry range of 2,350 miles (3,800km). Alternatively, fitting the D-704 "buddy" pack to the centreline station enables one Skyhawk to refuel another.

Above: Test examples of the "Snakeye" retarded bomb are seen on the centreline of a Skyhawk. Below: Two A-4L Skyhawks bailed to Flight Systems demonstrate "Buddy" aerial refuelling technique.

2

Single-seaters for Home and Abroad

URING A production run which spanned more than 25 years, it was hardly surprising that the number of variations on the Skyhawk theme was large, more than 20 derivatives having appeared by the time production ceased in early 1979 when the last A-4M was handed over to the US Marine Corps. Some of these derivatives were new-build aircraft while others arose as a result of extensive rework and/or remanufacture and it would seem advisable to examine these two categories individually, starting with the new-build subtypes.

Mention has already been made of the A4D-1 (later A-4A), 146 production examples of this version following on from the pre-production batch. Even as the A4D-1 was engaged in development flying, so had the A4D-2 (later A-4B) made its debut, taking to the air for the first time on 26 March 1956.

Instantly recognisable by virtue of being the first Skyhawk with the now familiar "tadpole" rudder, the A4D-2 also introduced several less obvious improvements. For instance, armament capability was upgraded to incorporate the Bullpup air-to-surface missile while combat radius undoubtedly benefitted from the provision of an in-flight refuelling probe. At a later date, this Skyhawk model also acquired the ability to serve as a tanker, a special centreline store being conceived by Douglas. Containing a hose and drogue assembly plus 300 US gal (1,136l) of fuel, the so-called "buddy" pack permitted the A4D-2 to transfer all its external fuel as well as half the internal fuel for a total of 1,300 US gal (4,925l) and it very quickly proved its worth, achieving the first "save" during the first major deployment.

Other changes were intended to eradicate some of the more unsatisfactory aspects of the original version, these resulting in the installation of a dual hydraulic system and provision of powered flying controls while the basic structure was also beefed up, permitting the maximum speed manoeuvre limit to rise to a creditable 7g.

Eventually, after some 18 months of flight testing, the A4D-2 began to enter service in September 1957. Early production examples joined VMA-211 and by the beginning of 1958 it was also in the process of equipping three Atlantic Fleet Naval Air Force (NavAirLant) units, namely VA-12, VA-83 and VA-86.

Heavily committed

By then, the Navy and Marine Corps were heavily committed to the Skyhawk and, more specifically, to the A4D-2 which eventually became the second most numerous variant, with 542 examples completed. Production then switched to the A4D-2N (later A-4C) which represented a significant improvement, largely as a result of the fact that it possessed a measure of all-weather attack potential arising from the decision to instal radar.

The unit chosen was the AN/APG-53A which was basically the brainchild of the Naval Avionics Facility at Indianapolis, where work on a simple radar ranging set had been in hand for some time. Despite the fact that, at just 90lbs (40.8kg), it was a lightweight unit, it was no lightweight in terms of capability. Surface mapping and ranging functions were performed by the APG-53 which also generated a vertical profilometer display, basically a rudimentary form of terrain avoidance which permitted pilots to fly fairly low and quite fast without having to worry too much about unplanned contact with terra firma.

Other new equipment included the AJB-3 low altitude bombing system/attitude and heading reference system (LABS/AHRS), the TPQ-10 blind bombing system, an automatic flight control system

McDONNELL DOUGLAS A-4M SKYHAWK CUTAWAY

1. Fixed in-flight refuelling probe.
2. Nose ECM recording and suppression aerials.
3. Angle Rate Bombing System (ARBS) laser seeker head.
4. Hinged nose compartment access door.
5. Laser seeker system electronics.
6. Electronics cooling air inlet.
7. Pitot tube.
8. Avionics access panel.
9. APN-153(V) navigation radar.
10. Lower TACAN aerial.
11. Communications electronics.
12. Cockpit front pressure bulkhead.
13. Pressurisation valve.
14. Windshield rain dispersal air duct.
15. Rudder pedals.
16. Angle-of-attack sensor.
17. Air conditioning refrigeration plant.
18. Nosewheel door.
19. Control system access.
20. Cockpit floor level.
21. Pilot's side console panel.
22. Engine throttle.
23. Control column.
24. Instrument panel shroud.
25. Head-up display (HUD).
26. Windscreen panels.
27. AIM-9L Sidewinder air-to-air missile.
28. Missile launch rail.
29. D-704 flight refuelling pack containing 300 US gal (135l).
30. Cockpit canopy cover.
31. Face blind firing handle.
32. Ejection seat headrest.
33. Safety harness.
34. McDonnell Douglas ESCAPAC IG-3 zero-zero ejection seat.
35. Anti-'g' valve.
36. Cockpit insulation and fragmentation blanket.
37. Rear pressure bulkhead.
38. Emergency canopy release handle.
39. Nose undercarriage leg strut.
40. Steering linkage.
41. Nosewheel.
42. Leg shortening link.
43. Hydraulic retraction strut.
44. Emergency wind-driven generator.
45. Port cannon muzzle.
46. Intake gun gas shield.
47. Port air intake.
48. Boundary layer splitter plate.
49. Self-sealing fuselage fuel cell, capacity 240 US gal (908l).
50. Fuel system piping.
51. Canopy hinge cover.
52. Starboard air intake duct.
53. Fuel system gravity filler cap.
54. UHF aerial.

55. Electronics cooling air inlet.
56. Engine-driven generator.
57. Constant-speed drive unit.
58. Bifurcated intake duct.
59. Reel type ammunition magazine (200 rounds per gun).
60. Intake compressor face.
61. Electrical system power amplifier.
62. Engine accessory drive gearbox.
63. Wing spar attachment fuselage double frame.
64. Engine mounting trunnion.
65. Engine fuel system access panel.
66. Pratt & Whitney J52-P-408 turbojet.
67. Dorsal avionics bays.
68. Compressor bleed air exhaust duct.
69. Upper TACAN aerial.
70. Starboard wing integral fuel tank (total wing tank capacity 560 US gal 2 120l).
71. Wing tank access panels.
72. Slat guide rails.
73. Starboard automatic leading-edge slat (open).
74. Wing fences.
75. Vortex generators.

76. Starboard navigation light.
77. Wing tip communications aerial.
78. Aileron horn balance.
79. Starboard aileron.
80. Split trailing-edge spoiler (open position).
81. Starboard split trailing-edge flap (down position).
82. Anti-collision light.
83. Cooling air exit louvres.
84. Rear fuselage double frame break point.
85. Engine firewall.
86. Cooling air intake.
87. VHF aerial.
88. Upper fuselage stringers.
89. Fin root dorsal fairing.
90. Remote compass flux valve.
91. Rear electronics bay cooling air inlet.
92. Fin rib construction.
93. Fin spar attachment joint.
94. Rudder hydraulic jack.
95. Artificial feel spring unit.
96. Pitot tube.
97. Fin tip ECM antenna housing.

98. Externally-braced rudder construction.
99. Fixed rudder tab.
100. Tail navigation light.
101. ECM antennae.
102. Tailplane trim jack.
103. Tailplane sealing plate.
104. Elevator hydraulic jack.
105. Tailpipe fairing.
106. Port elevator.
107. All moving tailplane construction.
108. Elevator horn balance.
109. Jet pipe exhaust nozzle.
110. Brake parachute housing for 16-ft (4.88m) diameter ribbon type chute.
111. Brake parachute release linkage.
112. Insulated jet pipe.
113. Electronics bay heat shield.
114. Rear electronics bay, automatic flight control system (AFCS).

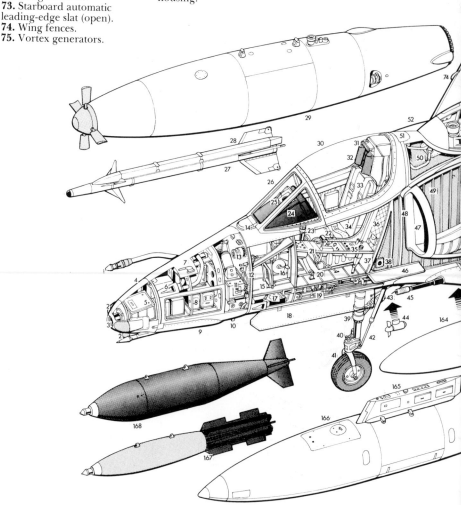

115. Port airbrake (open).
116. JATO bottle attachment hardpoints.
117. Airbrake hydraulic jack.
118. 2.65 US gal (10l) liquid oxygen converter (LOX).
119. Arrester hook (down position).
120. Arrester hook hydraulic jack.
121. Control cable runs.
122. Inertial platform.
123. Ventral pressure refuelling connection.
124. Central hydraulic flap drive linkage.
125. Port upper surface spoiler.
126. Spoiler hydraulic jack.
127. Ventral anti-collision light.
128. Wing rib construction.

129. Stringer construction.
130. Port wing integral fuel tank (single tank tip-to-tip).
131. Rear spar.
132. Port split trailing edge flap.
133. Port aileron construction.
134. Aileron trim tab.
135. Tip fairing.
136. Aileron horn balance.
137. Wing tip antenna fairing.
138. Port navigation light.
139. LAU-10A Zuni rocket launcher.
140. 5-in (12.7-cm) folding fin rocket.
141. AGM-12 Bullpup air-to-ground missile.
142. Missile launch rail.
143. Outboard wing pylon (1,000 lb 454 kg capacity).

144. Port automatic leading-edge slat (open).
145. Wing fences.
146. Vortex generators.
147. Aileron control rod linkage.
148. Leading edge ribs.
149. Wing centre spar.
150. Main undercarriage hydraulic retraction jack.
151. Undercarriage leg pivot mounting.

152. Slat guide rail fuel sealing can.
153. Port mainwheel.
154. Mainwheel door.
155. Position of landing lamp on starboard mainwheel door.
156. Approach lights.
157. Retractable catapult hook.

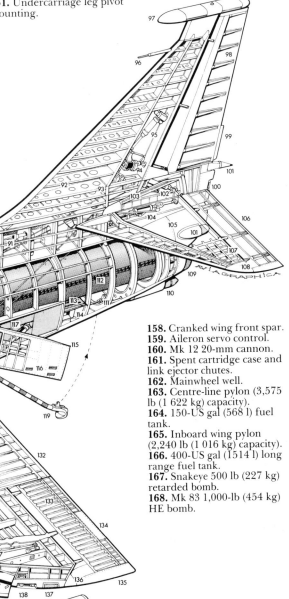

158. Cranked wing front spar.
159. Aileron servo control.
160. Mk 12 20-mm cannon.
161. Spent cartridge case and link ejector chutes.
162. Mainwheel well.
163. Centre-line pylon (3,575 lb (1 622 kg) capacity).
164. 150-US gal (568 l) fuel tank.
165. Inboard wing pylon (2,240 lb (1 016 kg) capacity).
166. 400-US gal (1514 l) long range fuel tank.
167. Snakeye 500 lb (227 kg) retarded bomb.
168. Mk 83 1,000-lb (454 kg) HE bomb.

Above: Immaculate in their blue and gold trim, the six A-4Fs of the Navy's Blue Angels aerobatic team plummet earthwards during a formation loop manoeuvre. The team also used a two-seat TA-4J.

(AFCS) and an airstream direction detector (ADD).

There was no prototype of the A4D-2N in the most widely accepted sense and it was the first production example which made the maiden flight on 21 August 1958, the forerunner of an eventual total of 638. By far the most numerous Skyhawk version, it was not in fact the most widely used (that distinction was claimed by the A-4B which flew with 35 Navy and 12 Marine Corps squadrons) but it did eventually build-up an impressive front-line service record with some 29 Navy and 11 Marine Corps light attack squadrons. In addition, it also equipped a handful of training units and a host of second-line and Reserve elements in a career spanning some 16 years. Today, although it no longer serves the US armed forces, the A-4C is still active overseas, most notably in Argentina, Malaysia and Singapore.

The A4D-2N entered service in March 1960 and,

once again, it was a Marine Corps unit which introduced the newest model, this distinction going to VMA-225 at Cherry Point MCAS, North Carolina. Subsequently, VA-192 became the first Navy squadron in May of the same year.

Neither the A4D-3 or the A4D-4 ever made it as far as the flight test stage. Essentially they were based on the A4D-2 and A4D-2N respectively and it should be noted that ten examples of the former sub-type were on order at one time. Had they gone ahead, they would have introduced a new engine.

The limited potential of the Wright J65 had for some time been a matter of some concern to both the Navy and Marine Corps which were anxious to switch to the Pratt & Whitney J52. As it transpired, cancellation of the A4D-3 and A4D-4 temporarily put paid to those aspirations and it was not until the A4D-5 that the switch was made.

In its initial guise as the J52-P-6, the Pratt & Whitney engine possessed a maximum static thrust rating of 8,500lb (3,855kg), identical to that achieved by the final J65-W-18 variant. However, the J52 was much less thirsty in terms of fuel consumption and substitution offered immediate benefits. Even more important was the new engine's potential for "growth", subsequent development eventually culminating in an increase in thrust of some 30 per cent.

Such improvements were, however, some way in the future when the J52 made its debut in the Skyhawk, a couple of A4D-2Ns (Bu.Nos. 148613-614) being modified on the production line to serve as A4D-5 (later A-4E) prototypes. First flown in prototype form on 12 July 1961, the A4D-5 also featured a greatly revised avionics suite, new items including Doppler radar, Tacan (tactical air navigation) equipment and a radar altimeter, while the LABS/AHRS package was updated to AJB-3A standard. Provision was made for another two stores stations, thus raising the number of weapons pylons to five—but this was not achieved without penalty, for the wing structure also required strengthening which inevitably led to a slight increase in empty weight.

Production began in earnest in 1962 with the first deliveries taking place in November of that year when VA-23 began converting from the A4D-2. For a time it looked as if the "echo" would be the last single-seat Skyhawk. As things turned out the exigencies of war provided an extended lease of life,

prolonging production of the A4D-5 until 1966 by which time some 497 examples had been turned out. Eventually, in a career which lasted until well into the 1970s, some 30 front-line Navy and Marine Corps squadrons utilised this derivative.

Winding down

Even as production of the A-4E was winding down, work was forging ahead on what was to be the last single-seat version to see service with the US Navy in an operational capacity, the A-4F. The final A-4E (Bu.No.152101) was subjected to production line modification in order to serve as a prototype, making its first flight on 31 August 1966. It was eventually followed down the line by 146 production articles.

Benefitting from the increased power of the J52-P-8A engine which was rated at 9,300lb st (4,218kg), the A-4F was perhaps the most drastic Skyhawk revamping to date, tangible evidence of this being the prominent dorsal "hump". Housing additional avionics gear, this was added to a considerable number of A-4Es as they underwent modernisation and modification programmes aimed at enhancing

Above: The front office of the Skyhawk also obeyed Heinemann's injunction to "keep it simple" as is clearly evident in this cockpit view of an early production example of the A4D-1.

capability. Subsequently 100 A-4Fs were fitted with the more powerful J52-P-401, which required slight modification to air intake geometry.

Armour protection was also provided while another measure which must have been warmly welcomed by pilots was the fitment of a zero-zero ejection seat. Wing spoilers also made their debut on the A-4F as did nose-wheel steering and low pressure tyres.

Entering service in the summer of 1967, A-4F transition was carried through remarkably quickly. By January 1968 six NavAirPac squadrons had been more or less completely equipped, and five of them were already en route to the Vietnam war zone in Tonkin Gulf.

VA-23 and VA-192 shared the distinction of introducing this Skyhawk model to combat when the first operational sorties were launched from the USS *Ticonderoga* on 26 January 1968. Within a month, three more A-4F squadrons had delivered their first ordnance loads, VA-93 and VA-212 entering the fray on 21 February and VA-113 following suit the next day.

During the next eight years, 11 front-line Navy squadrons operated the A-4F at various times. It served only with elements of the Pacific Fleet, and its operational career with the Navy did not terminate until December 1975. This did not quite mark the end of the line for the A-4F, as surviving examples were reassigned to a few USMC squadrons with which it remained in use until supplanted by the A-4M. Thereafter, A-4Fs were passed on to second-line Marine Reserve force units.

The next three single-seat models—the A-4G, A-4H and A-4K—were all earmarked for overseas operators and were manufactured in only modest quantities. Full details of these are given in the chapter which examines export Skyhawks in more detail, but, broadly speaking, Australia's A-4G was virtually identical to the A-4E but the A-4H broke new ground in that it introduced several new features at Israel's request.

Revised fin

A revised square-tipped fin and rudder assembly was one of the key recognition points but the A-4H also featured a braking parachute as standard.

Beneath the skin, armament also changed, the Colt Mk.12 cannon giving way to a pair of DEFA 30-mm guns, each with 150 rounds of ammunition. Finally, the A-4K was perhaps something of a hybrid, marrying some features of the A-4H to what was basically an A-4F airframe. Thus, it inherited the modified fin and braking parachute from the A-4H while also featuring the A-4F's dorsal avionics pack. A different radio fit was also specified by New Zealand.

The next major derivative marked a resumption of procurement of single-seat Skyhawks by the USA and, more specifically, the Marines. At one time, it was intended that they would also obtain Vought's A-7 Corsair II, a quite sophisticated type which was perhaps too refined for the Marines who really needed something much more basic. Super systems are all very well but in the type of war that the Marines are traditionally called upon to fight the A-7 looked like an expensive luxury, possessing qualities which were far in excess of what the Corps actually wanted.

In the end the service got its way and a new variant of the Skyhawk resulted, in the shape of the A-4M which first flew on 10 April 1970. Deliveries to

Below: In recent times, the Skyhawk has been extensively used as an "aggressor" aircraft by various US Navy units engaged in air combat training. This pair of A-4Fs are from VF-126 at Miramar.

VMA-324 at Beaufort, South Carolina started just over a year later.

A distillation of all the best features of preceding Skyhawks, the A-4M was easily the most capable model, as well as the most powerful by virtue of the J52-P-408A which generated 11,200lbs (5,080kg) of thrust. A square-capped fin, similar to that of the A-4H/K, later provided a convenient anchor point for ECM equipment and the A-4M also introduced a much revised canopy giving enhanced all-round vision. A "bent" flight refuelling probe was fitted to minimise interference with the radar, and the aircraft had a braking chute, additional ammunition capacity (at 200 rounds per gun, exactly twice that of its predecessors), self-start capability, a new gunsight and a ram air turbine for emergency power supply.

Avionics were also the subject of improvement and post-production modification has resulted in the A-4M "sprouting" numerous additional appendages since it entered service, the fin-top "bullet" being one of the more obvious growths. Many of these 'add-ons' are ECM-related, apart from the cluster of "bumps and bulges" which now surround the nose. These are associated with the Hughes Angle Rate Bombing Systems (ARBS).

A valuable adjunct which incorporates a laser seeker head, ARBS enables Skyhawks to employ laser-guided weapons such as the AGM-65E Maverick for precision attacks on "hard" targets. Testing of ARBS was accomplished during the latter half of the 1970s; at one time it looked as though aircraft with this package would be known as A-4Ys but in the event the A-4M designation was retained. ARBS was installed on quite a few new-build Skyhawks as well as being retrospectively fitted to older examples.

Despite enjoying a particularly lengthy production run, only 158 A-4Ms were completed between 1970 and 27 February 1979 when the final example—coincidentally the last Skyhawk built—was formally handed over to the Marines. Resplendent in a special colour scheme, Skyhawk No.2960 (Bu.No.160264) was immediately assigned to VMA-331 at MCAS Cherry Point.

Israel's A-4N and Kuwait's A-4KU

Two other new-build single-seaters also deserve mention, the A-4N and the A-4KU. Both evolved in response to export orders placed in the 1970s, Israel's A-4N being basically similar to the A-4M but with a much revised nav/attack system. Key elements of this are a Lear-Siegler digital computer, a Singer vertical platform and an Elliott Automation head-up display (HUD) unit. The A-4N was produced in concert with the A-4M and additional details pertaining to quantity may be found elsewhere. The final new-build export sub-type was the A-4KU for Kuwait and this too was based on the A-4M, the 30 examples being among the last Skyhawks built.

Although by no means as prolific as the new-build

versions, the various remanufacture and rebuild projects are an important part of the Skyhawk saga and a substantial number of aircraft were given this treatment in order to both extend their service lives and enhance capability. Five basic variants evolved in this fashion, all bar one arising to satisfy export customers, and it is probably best to consider them chronologically, starting with the A-4P which made its debut in 1966 when an initial batch of 25 entered service with the Argentine Air Force. A second, identically-sized, batch followed in the 1970s but it appears that the extent of modification was small, a belief supported by the fact that the FAA has always referred to them as A-4Bs. Further details relating to

these aircraft may be found in the chapters dealing with export aircraft and the Skyhawk's combat record.

The next major refurbishment project was rather more ambitious and certainly much more noticeable, involving exactly 100 A-4Cs. Making its first flight in modified form on 21 August 1969, the A-4L was essentially kitted out with a new avionics suite similar to that of the A-4F and featuring the dorsal "hump" introduced by that model. That appears to have been the limit of modernisation, since all 100 aircraft retained the original Wright J65 engine and the three stores stations.

Apart from the prototype conversion, responsibil-

Below: Production of new-build Skyhawks eventually terminated in February 1979 when Bu.No. 160264 was handed over to the Marines at Palmdale. To mark the occasion, it wore a special colour scheme.

ity for the A-4L was entrusted to the Navy's own rework facilities, using kits supplied by the manufacturer. This version entered service with the Navy Reserve shortly before the end of 1969. Eventually, most of the Navy squadrons which used the A-4L progressed to early models of the Corsair while their Marine counterparts picked up J52-powered Skyhawks. For the A-4L, this meant assignment to the regular force, some examples finding their way to Fleet Composite Squadrons (VC), but all had been retired by the summer of 1976.

Argentina was also the customer for the next version, the A-4Q. This, too, was essentially a revamped A-4B, 16 aircraft being delivered to that nation's naval air arm in 1971 for service from the aircraft carrier *25 de Mayo*. Again, modification appears to have been minimal in nature.

Major changes

Just two years later, Singapore's A-4S made its debut but this time the degree of modification was extensive, with well over 100 major changes being made. All of the 40 aircraft were A-4Bs taken from long-term desert storage, Lockheed Aircraft Services converting the first eight in California while the balance were modified in Singapore. Key aspects of the remanufacture process involved fitment of 30-mm Aden cannon, provision of a braking parachute, substitution of the 8,100lb st (3,674kg) Wright J65-W-20 and installation of a far more modern nav/attack package.

More recently, Singapore has decided to invest still more heavily in the Skyhawk, acquiring 70 A-4Cs and 16 TA-4Bs from the storage facility at Davis-Monthan in the early 1980s. Updating of these aircraft has resulted in the A-4S-1 and an allied TA-4S-1 trainer. New avionics, complete rewiring and stronger stores stations are major aspects of the rework which is being undertaken in-country and which should result in about 50 aircraft joining Singapore's steadily expanding inventory.

The most recent Skyhawk modification project—but almost certainly not the last—was handled by Grumman at the behest of Malaysia which purchased 88 A-4C/Ls. These aircraft were used to "produce" 34 single-seat A-4PTMs plus some two-seaters. Once again, remanufacture was extensive. However, budgetary limitations meant that the extent of updating was less ambitious than at first hoped.

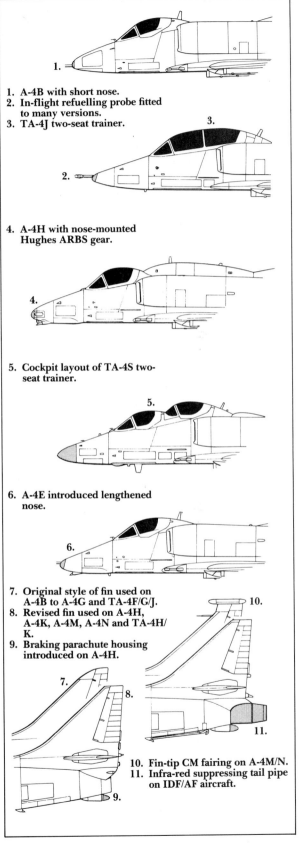

1. A-4B with short nose.
2. In-flight refuelling probe fitted to many versions.
3. TA-4J two-seat trainer.
4. A-4H with nose-mounted Hughes ARBS gear.
5. Cockpit layout of TA-4S two-seat trainer.
6. A-4E introduced lengthened nose.
7. Original style of fin used on A-4B to A-4G and TA-4F/G/J.
8. Revised fin used on A-4H, A-4K, A-4M, A-4N and TA-4H/K.
9. Braking parachute housing introduced on A-4H.
10. Fin-tip CM fairing on A-4M/N.
11. Infra-red suppressing tail pipe on IDF/AF aircraft.

3

Two-seaters for Training

ALTHOUGH manufactured in far fewer numbers, trainer versions of the Skyhawk still accounted for a respectable proportion of the overall production run, about 555 being completed between 1965 and 1978. In view of the type's widespread employment by Navy and Marine Corps units it is perhaps surprising that it took some ten years to get around to designing and developing a two-seater, especially as the TA-4 did achieve considerable success. It still has a very important part to play in producing today's naval aviator.

Development was actually initiated in response to a 1964 Navy request for two prototypes of an operational trainer derivative. Initially, this was allocated the designation TA-4E and the first prototype duly got airborne on 30 June 1965. However, since it utilised the J52-P-8A engine and a number of other features of the A-4F, the designation was very soon changed to TA-4F. Navy enthusiasm resulted in a succession of orders for this version and 239 were eventually built before production switched to the TA-4J.

As it turned out, many TA-4Fs were later modified to TA-4J standard but although most, if not all, TA-4Fs began life with a brace of Colt Mk.12 cannon, it was by no means uncommon for these to be deleted. However, it should be emphasised that deletion of the guns does not necessarily turn a TA-4F into a TA-4J—that only occurs when the associated nav/attack system is removed.

Aside from internal avionics, the basic two-seat Skyhawk required a 28inch (71cm) "stretch" to accommodate a second cockpit in tandem, this being achieved at some penalty in terms of fuselage fuel capacity, a loss of 136 US gal (515l) to be precise. However, since the TA-4F was mainly intended to operate with US-based fleet replacement squadrons, this was not a matter of great concern.

The first unit to take delivery of the TA-4F was VA-125 at Lemoore in May 1966 and other early

Above: Poised seemingly motionless above the flight deck of one of the Navy's large carriers, this two-seat TA-4J from VT-7 at Meridian, Mississippi, looks well set to make the "perfect trap".

production examples soon found their way to VA-44 of the Atlantic Fleet. Another early recipient was the US Marine Corps, several Headquarters and Maintenance Squadrons (H&MS) acquiring this model for a variety of tasks which included high-speed forward air control (FAC). In due course, the TA-4F became the only two-seater to be used in combat, H&MS units at Da Nang and Chu Lai operating in support of Marine attack and fighter attack squadrons from late 1967.

Non-combatant

For the most part the two-seaters were non-combatant but they did incorporate a fairly comprehensive bag of avionics, plus controls and displays for the APG-53A terrain clearance radar and the AJB-3A bombing system which were installed in the front cockpit only. Other items like the APN-141 radar altimeter were duplicated.

In contrast, the second major two-seat derivative was considerably less complex. This was the TA-4J,

Above: Carrying a mixture of fuel tanks, bombs and Bullpup air-to-surface missiles, an early production TA-4F illustrates this version's ability to operate effectively in a combat role.

which was, from the outset, intended to satisfy Navy advanced flying training requirements. First flown in May 1969, production continued until no fewer than 292 had been completed, although a small number of these were diverted to Israel. Since the TA-4J was not expected to be used in a combat capacity nor as a weapons trainer, it follows that the nav/attack system was deleted, the resultant weight saving permitting a switch to the less powerful J52-P-6 engine.

VT-21 at Kingsville, Texas was the first squadron to receive the TA-4J in June 1969, the new trainer initially supplanting and eventually replacing the vintage TAF/TF-9J Cougar with this unit and with VT-22 and VT-23 at the same base. Other key training centres which received Skyhawks in the first

half of the 1970s were Chase Field, Texas (VT-24/25); Pensacola, Florida (VT-4/86) and Meridian, Mississippi (VT-7). Quite a few examples of the TA-4J eventually joined regular Fleet squadrons like VF-126 at Miramar; VC-10 at Guantanamo Bay, Cuba and RVAH-3 at Key West, to be employed on a mix of training and support functions for the front-line forces.

Although the number of 'new-build' trainers produced for overseas customers was small—just 22 to be precise—a brief summary is probably in order here although further details may be found in a later chapter. Variants comprise the TA-4G for the Royal Australian Navy, the TA-4H for Israel, the TA-4K

Below: A trio of TA-4J Skyhawks from VT-24 at Chase Field salute four former presidents in a fly-past at Mount Rushmore. All three aircraft feature the usual white overall trainer colour scheme.

for New Zealand and the TA-4KU for Kuwait, quantities involved being two, ten, four and six respectively. Needless to say, configurations varied but these aircraft generally equated closely to the standard of the single-seaters supplied to the respective air arms with regard to avionics and armament capability.

Regarding modified aircraft, the TA-4F served as a basis for two particularly interesting derivatives, the Navy's EA-4F and the Marine Corps' OA-4M. Only four EA-4Fs were "produced" for service with ECM "aggressor" squadron VAQ-33, initially from Norfolk and, more recently, from Key West. Details of the aircraft involved appear in the appendices, and suffice to say that modification was accomplished over a four-year period from 1970. One was destroyed in the early 1980s and this does not seem to have been replaced.

Although by no means as extensively modified as some other VAQ-33 aircraft, the EA-4Fs do feature special wiring for simulator and chaff pods and can carry jammers. For the most part, though, they serve as missile "simulators", presumably duplicating weapons such as Exocet and Harpoon and providing Navy surface combatants with experience of dealing with the threat posed by these missiles.

The OA-4M is rather more numerous, with 23 aircraft being brought to this configuration in the late 1970s and early 1980s for service in the tactical control mission with elements of the USMC. Modification was accomplished under Navy auspices at Pensacola, Florida and the first example made its maiden flight from there on 23 May 1978. It subsequently spent some time with the Naval Air Test Center at Patuxent River. Delivery of "production"

conversions began in late 1979 to H&MS-32 at Cherry Point, and other squadrons with this unique variant are H&MS-12 at Iwakuni and H&MS-13 at El Toro.

Incorporating an avionics "hump" reminiscent of that introduced by the A-4F, key aspects of the modification effort for the OA-4M related to installation of ARC-159 UHF communications gear; VHF radio for air-ground communications; ARN-118 Tacan; ALQ-126 ECM; KY-28 secure voice system and ARL-45/50 radar threat warning system. Fin and nose ESM "caps", like those of the A-4M, are also fitted and all 23 aircraft were delivered in the current "low-viz" tactical camouflage.

The TA-4S-1 and TA-4PTM

Finally, two other Skyhawk trainers deserve brief mention, both originating from remanufacture and both destined for overseas air arms. Arguably the oddest-looking Skyhawk of all, the TA-4S (and the later TA-4S-1) was the brainchild of Lockheed Aircraft Services—McDonnell Douglas would surely have done it differently had they been behind this project—and features individual canopies rather than a single hood over the two cockpits. Seven aircraft were produced initially with a follow-on batch of at least eight TA-4S-1s, which are now in service. Malaysia's six TA-4PTMs were converted by Grumman and are basically comparable with all the two-seaters that have gone before as far as physical appearance is concerned.

Below: Trailing flame and smoke, a 2.75-inch unguided Zuni aerial rocket streaks away from a TA-4F Skyhawk of USMC attack training squadron VMAT-102 during a sortie from MCAS Yuma in Arizona.

Above: Marine technicians get to grips with some of the avionics equipment which is packed into the Skyhawk. Clearly visible is the laser seeker head which forms an integral part of the Hughes Angle-Rate Bombing System as fitted to the A-4M.

Above: The standard gull grey and white Navy colour scheme is worn by this otherwise anomymous A-4B being readied for flight.

Left: Two A-4Cs of VA-112 fly in fairly close formation while assigned to Carrier Air Wing 16 on the USS *Ticonderoga* in 1969.

A-4C Skyhawk 149532/NH-312 saw combat action with VA-144 from the USS Kitty Hawk during 1966–67.

Typical of the TA-4J two-seat trainer variant, this aircraft displays the markings of VT-86 at Pensacola, Florida.

The Black Lancer insignia of VA-64.

This device adorned VA-212's Skyhawks.

Carrying Bullpup ASMs and conventional bombs, A-4M 158412/WE-11 is from VMA-214.

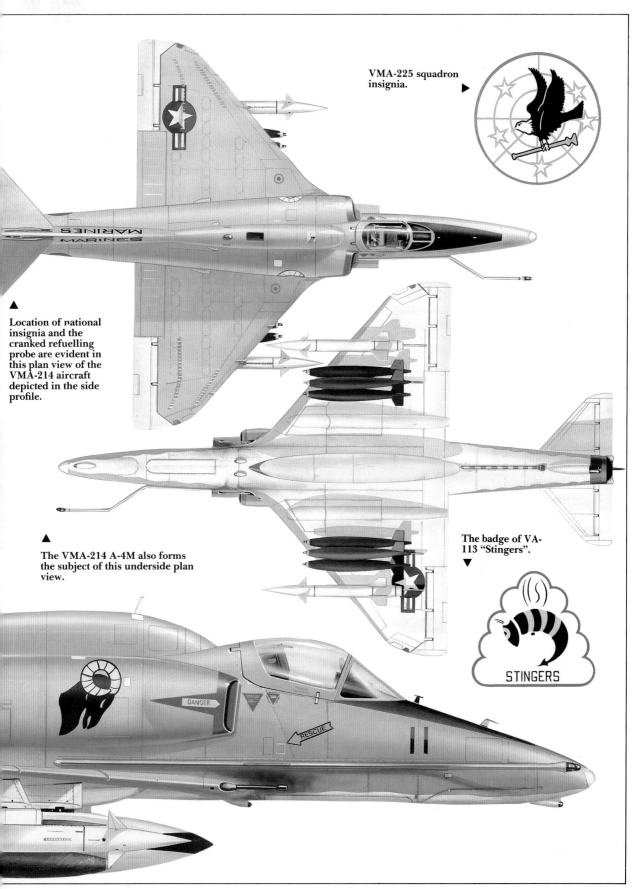

VMA-225 squadron insignia. ▶

▲
Location of national insignia and the cranked refuelling probe are evident in this plan view of the VMA-214 aircraft depicted in the side profile.

▲
The VMA-214 A-4M also forms the subject of this underside plan view.

The badge of VA-113 "Stingers". ▼

STINGERS

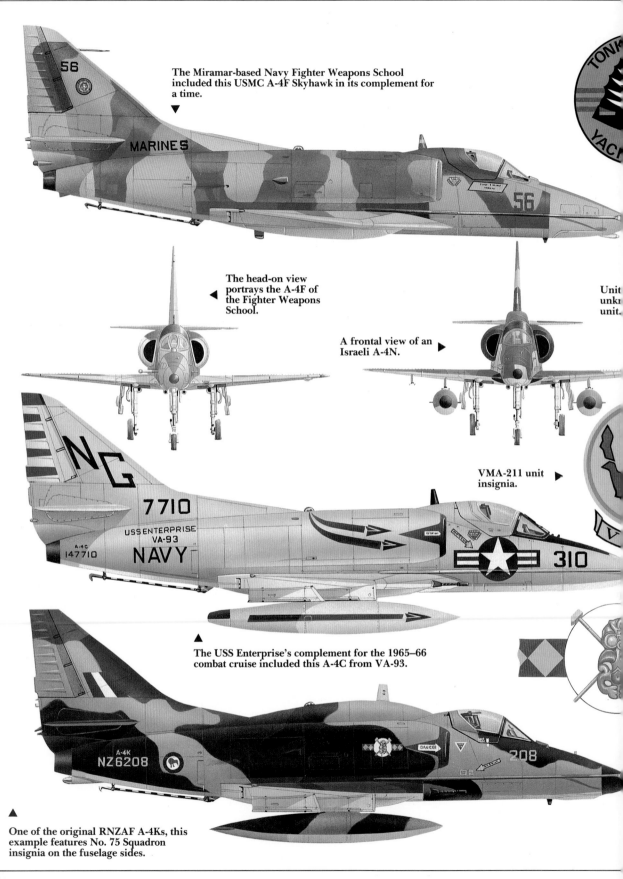

The Miramar-based Navy Fighter Weapons School included this USMC A-4F Skyhawk in its complement for a time.
▼

The head-on view portrays the A-4F of the Fighter Weapons School.
◄

Unit
unkr
unit.

A frontal view of an Israeli A-4N. ►

VMA-211 unit insignia. ►

▲
The USS Enterprise's complement for the 1965–66 combat cruise included this A-4C from VA-93.

▲
One of the original RNZAF A-4Ks, this example features No. 75 Squadron insignia on the fuselage sides.

This unusual badge was applied to aircraft flown by pilots who had been rescued from the Tonkin Gulf.

An infra-red suppressing exhaust nozzle has been fitted to this Israeli A-4N Skyhawk II.

of an
AF

Unit markings of another unknown IDF/AF unit.

Upper wing markings and the original style of refuelling probe may be seen in this plan view of an IDF/AF A-4N.

etail of No. 75 quadron insignia.

No. 805 Squadron, Royal Australian Navy.

AIM-9 Sidewinder air-to-air missiles are carried by this A-4G of the Australian Navy's No. 805 Squadron.

Malaysia's A-4PTM Skyhawks all feature a distinctive camouflage pattern, as do the TA-4PTMs.

This Singaporean A-4S carries No. 143 Squadron's insignia on the forward fuselage section.

No. 143 Squadron, Singapore Air Force.

Nose detail of FAA A-4C C-321. Ship silhouette is for HMS Invincible; badge is of Grupo 4 and Falklands map also appears.

National insignia was displayed by FAA aircraft at the time of the Falklands conflict as can be seen on A-4C Skyhawk C-321 of the IV Brigada Aerea.

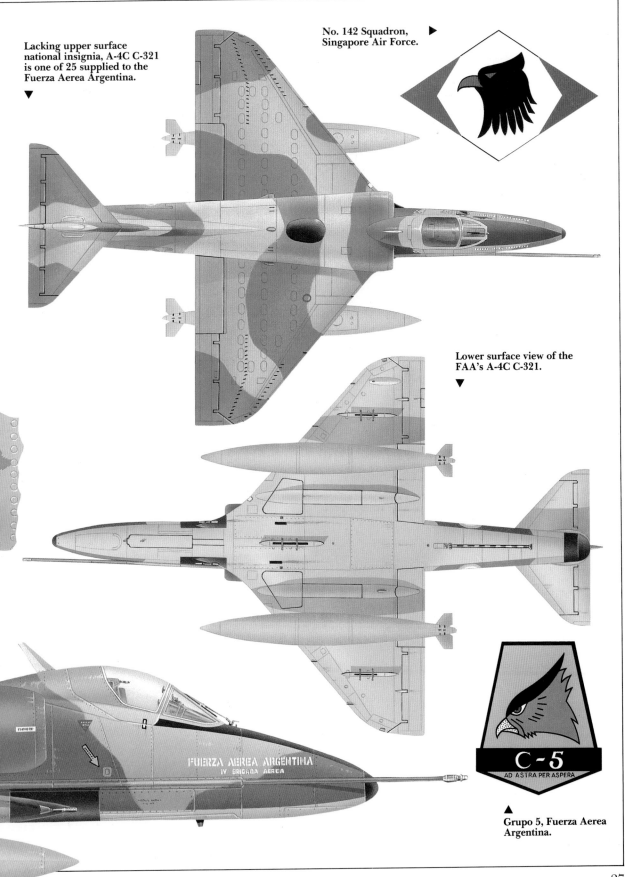

Lacking upper surface national insignia, A-4C C-321 is one of 25 supplied to the Fuerza Aerea Argentina. ▼

No. 142 Squadron, Singapore Air Force. ▶

Lower surface view of the FAA's A-4C C-321. ▼

FUERZA AEREA ARGENTINA
IV BRIGADA AEREA

C-5
AD ASTRA PER ASPERA

▲ Grupo 5, Fuerza Aerea Argentina.

Above: Rear-seat view of a VAQ-33 EA-4F from another EA-4F of the same unit. Employed in the ECM "aggressor" role, VAQ-33 has operated Skyhawks since about 1970.

Above: with the unit badge "passed" by the censor an IDF-AF A-4N returns from a training sortie, streaming a cruciform braking parachute. Note the infra-red suppressing tail pipe.

Right: Apart from its "Firebirds" insignia and data block, there are no visible clues to differentiate the EA-4F variant used by VAQ-33 from a standard TA-4F two-seater.

4

Skyhawks for Export

AS FAR AS the export market is concerned, despite the fact that it was a relatively inexpensive machine both to buy and operate, the Skyhawk did not score heavily when it came to the sale of new-build aircraft. Indeed, less than ten per cent of total production was undertaken to satisfy export contracts, just 277 new aircraft finding their way overseas. Even then, customers were never easy to find and the Skyhawk had actually been in production for over ten years with some 2,000 examples completed before the first export order was secured in the mid-1960s.

By that time, however, early production variants had begun to disappear from the US inventory, being consigned to storage in the Arizona desert as more modern equipment reached the front-line. Since these redundant aircraft could be obtained relatively cheaply and were still quite potent machines, it was hardly surprising that they interested overseas customers. Argentina's Air Force was the first to acquire A-4s from this source.

Ultimately, the disposal of aircraft considered sur-

plus to US requirements extended to around 400 Skyhawks but not all were destined to fly again. Taking the customers chronologically rather than alphabetically (although Argentina does qualify as the starting point on both scores), all 91 aircraft received by this nation were former USN/MC examples although the extent of remanufacture was modest. Nevertheless, the transfer of these Skyhawks did result in two new designations, these being A-4P and A-4Q. Deliveries took place over a period of about ten years.

Argentine aircraft

The first contract placed was for 25 aircraft for the *Fuerza Aerea Argentina* (FAA or Argentine Air Force), these being given the serial numbers C-201 to C-225. All were former A-4Bs, the first example making its maiden flight on the last day of 1965. It was not however until October 1966 that deliveries got under way, the intervening period being spent in crew training in the USA. Officially, these Skyhawks took the designation A-4P but this appears to have been ignored by Argentina where they have always been (and still are) referred to as A-4Bs.

Another batch of 25 ex-Navy A-4Bs (also designated A-4Ps) was delivered between late 1969 and early 1970, these adopting serial numbers which followed on from the initial group (C-226 to C-250). Finally, in the latter half of 1974, 25 surplus A-4Cs were removed from storage and ferried to Lockheed Aircraft Services at Ontario, California for refurbishing. Given the serial numbers C-301 to C-325, they retained the A-4C designation.

As far as operational service is concerned, the first 50 aircraft all found their way to *Grupo 5 de Caza* at Villa Reynolds, where they equipped the IV and V *Escuadrones de Caza Bombardeo*. It was with this unit that the A-4B/A-4P eventually saw combat, many of the FAA's surviving Skyhawks being committed to

Below: Variations in the camouflage pattern and physical differences between single and two-seat Skyhawks are evident in this view of the first examples of New Zealand's A-4K and TA-4K.

action in the 1982 battle for the Falklands.

The 19 or so survivors of the 25 A-4Cs delivered in 1976 also made an important contribution to Argentina's war effort, operating with *Grupo 4 de Caza's III Escuadrone de Caza Bombardeo* which was normally stationed at Los Tamarindos. Fuller details of the part played in the battle for the Falklands by the FAA Skyhawks follow later.

The second major element of Argentina's armed forces to operate Skyhawks was the *Comando Aviacion Naval Argentina* (CANA or Argentine Naval Aviation

Command) which obtained 16 refurbished A-4Bs in 1971-72 and assigning serial numbers in the block 0654 to 0669. These were mainly intended for use from Argentina's solitary aircraft carrier, the ARA *25 de Mayo*, small numbers routinely being embarked for sea-going operations alongside other types like the S-2 Tracker and the Sikorsky S-61D-4. Unlike the FAA, however, CANA preferred to utilise the official Department of Defense designation of A-4Q when referring to these aircraft.

Initially delivered to No.2 *Escuadrilla de Caza y Ataque* at Comandante Espora, Bahia Blanca, Buenos Aires, they were soon reassigned to the 3rd *Escuadrilla* in what was essentially a "paper" transfer. The survivors were still active with No.3 Escuadrilla at the time of the altercation with Great Britain and did achieve some success despite the fact that CANA was only able to muster eight serviceable aircraft at the start of the conflict—a number which had literally been halved by the end.

Moving on to Australia, this country became the first customer for new-build Skyhawks during the mid-1960s. Intended for service with VF-805 squadron from the carrier HMAS *Melbourne* in the attack/interceptor role, they were the forerunners of an initial batch of eight A-4G single-seaters and two TA-4G two-seaters. Respective first flights by these models were made on 19 July and 7 August 1967.

Navy channels

Procured via US Navy channels, they were allocated Bureau Numbers 154903-910 (A-4G) and 154911-912 (TA-4G), and given the prefix "N13" in Royal Australian Navy service. Normally shore-based at Nowra, New South Wales when not embarked, they were augmented by a batch of ex-USN A-4F and TA-4F Skyhawks in 1971. Previous identities of the A-4Fs were 155051, 155052, 155055, 155056, 155061, 155062, 155063, and 155069 while the pair of TA-4Fs were 154647 and 154648. Once again, the prefix "N13" was adopted in RAN useage.

In addition to VF-805, some aircraft were also assigned to VC-724 squadron at Nowra, this functioning as a training and trials unit – in consequence, it operated all the two-seaters as well as at least one single-seater. Eventually, following the retirement of the *Melbourne* during the mid-1980s, the survivors were transferred to New Zealand.

In terms of quantity, Israel is far and away the most important overseas operator. Unfortunately, that nation's excellent, near impenetrable security blanket means that it is impossible to categorise those units which have used the type and almost as difficult to be specific as to just how many A-4s have seen service with the Israel Defence Force/Air Force (IDF/AF).

New-build aircraft like the A-4H, TA-4H and A-4N are fairly straightforward to document – the problem arises with those which were obtained second-hand during the October 1973 war when a substantial number of US Navy A-4Es were hurriedly ferried to Israel to replace combat losses. Further confusion arises from the fact that the three-digit IDF/AF serial numbers are allocated randomly so there are no clues to be found there either.

However, it is generally accepted that the total quantity supplied to Israel is around the 300 mark.

Below: Almost certainly photographed at Palmdale, California soon after it was rolled out in summer 1972, Bu.No. 158726 was the first of 117 A-4Ns built for Israel's Defence Force/Air Force.

New-build examples account for 217, a figure made up of 90 A-4H and 117 A-4N single-seaters plus ten TA-4H two-seaters. In addition, most sources tend to support the belief that approximately 60 A-4Es found their way to the IDF/AF as well as 17 or 18 TA-4Js, all of which were former US Navy machines.

Deliveries kicked-off with the A-4H which made its maiden flight on 27 October 1967. The first examples were handed over soon afterwards and production of this sub-type continued until the early 1970s. Ten broadly-similar TA-4H two-seaters were also manufactured to fulfil the training function, this derivative flying for the first time on 15 April 1969.

Attention switched

With A-4H production complete, attention then switched to the A-4N which first flew in June 1972. Successful testing of this variant cleared the way for deliveries to begin later that year. Palmdale was still busily building A-4Ns when the loss of no fewer than 50 assorted Skyhawks during the Yom Kippur war of 1973 prompted an urgent request from Israel for additional aircraft. The US response was commendably swift, an infusion of at least three dozen A-4Es augmenting an initial batch – allegedly of about 25 aircraft – supplied in 1969. But, with the A-4E no longer featuring prominently in the US Navy line-

Above: National insignia applied to RNZAF Skyhawks was eventually changed in favour of a roundel showing the kiwi while some aircraft also gained No. 75 Squadron's insignia on the intake sides.

up, suitable specimens were not easy to find. The result was that even elite units like the US Navy's "Top Gun Flight" at Miramar were denuded of aircraft.

In more recent years, the number of aircraft in Israeli hands has been in decline, combat and routine operational attrition bringing about a reduction in numbers, as has the availability of more potent equipment like the Kfir and the F-16. As the requirement for the Skyhawk diminished, Israel began casting around for suitable markets for the surplus aircraft; evidence of success in this endeavour being provided by the transfer of some Skyhawks to Indonesia. It also appears that pilots of Argentina's CANA have been looking eastwards, but at present it seems unlikely that that country will get the opportunity to upgrade to the rather more potent A-4E/H variants.

New Zealand became the fourth Skyhawk customer in 1970 when it took delivery of a total of 14 examples. Made up of ten single-seat A-4Ks (first flight 10 November 1969) and four two-seat TA-4K (first flight 5 December 1969), all 14 were earmarked for service with No.75 Squadron at Ohakea. Allocated US Navy Bureau Numbers in the block

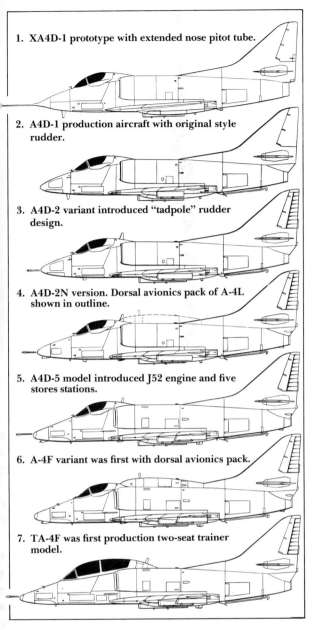

1. XA4D-1 prototype with extended nose pitot tube.

2. A4D-1 production aircraft with original style rudder.

3. A4D-2 variant introduced "tadpole" rudder design.

4. A4D-2N version. Dorsal avionics pack of A-4L shown in outline.

5. A4D-5 model introduced J52 engine and five stores stations.

6. A-4F variant was first with dorsal avionics pack.

7. TA-4F was first production two-seat trainer model.

157904 to 157913, the A-4Ks were given the RNZAF serial numbers NZ6201 to NZ6210 while the TA-4Ks (Bu.Nos. 157914-157917) became NZ6251 to NZ6254.

Attrition has been slight, only one of each sub-type having been lost in 17 years of service. The RNZAF nevertheless received an infusion of "new" equipment in July 1984 when it took delivery of the ten surviving RAN A-4Gs and TA-4Gs, using these to equip the re-activated No.2 Squadron, also at Oha-kea. Aircraft involved in this transfer comprised 154903, 154904, 154905, 154908, 155052, 155061, 155063 and 155069 which adopted RNZAF mark-ings as NZ6211 to NZ6218 respectively while TA-4Gs 154912 became NZ6255 and NZ6256 respectively.

An ambitious and ongoing modernisation pro-gramme embracing all 22 RNZAF Skyhawks should result in them remaining active for the foreseeable future, with new avionics equipment incorporated in concert with the provision of chaff/flare dispensers and a braking parachute.

"Brand-new"

By way of contrast, all the aircraft which have found their way into Singaporean service have been obtained second-hand although extensive remanu-facture has resulted in their being what may effec-tively be described as "brand-new" machines. For the first few years after its formation in 1968, the Republic of Singapore Air Force was heavily depen-dent on Britain as a source of combat aircraft and it was not until 1972 that it began to look elsewhere for such equipment. In that year, an order was placed for an initial batch of Skyhawks and delivery of these began in the latter half of 1973.

All were former US Navy A-4Bs taken from storage at Davis-Monthan AFB, and responsibility for rework was entrusted to Lockheed Aircraft Ser-vices which "produced" an initial batch of eight single-seat A-4Ss at Ontario, California where the first example made its maiden flight on 14 July 1973. Thereafter, the task of conversion switched to Singa-pore – but still under LAS auspices – where a further 32 single-seaters were given the treatment between 1974 and 1976.

Modification was extensive, with a considerable amount of British equipment including 30-mm Aden cannon and a Ferranti lead-computing sight being specified. At the same time, spoilers and a braking parachute were fitted as standard. The resulting A-4S entered service with No.142 "Gryphon" Squadron at Tengah in 1974 and the same base is also home for No.143 "Phoenix" Squad-ron which formed in 1975.

Initial training was undertaken in the USA with the first eight aircraft at Lemoore NAS, California, this base also providing a temporary home for the first three TA-4S two-seaters which were also "pro-duced" at Ontario. Getting airborne for its maiden flight on 21 February 1975, the TA-4S is without doubt the most distinctive trainer variant in that it employs separate hoods for the tandem cockpits, bestowing a somewhat bizarre appearance. Some 28 inches (71cm) longer than the more conventional A-4S, the TA-4S retains full combat capability and the original three examples were augmented by four more from the Singapore "line" at a later date. These were distributed between the two operational units. Details of serial numbers may be found elsewhere.

Experience gained

Operational experience gained with the A-4S was no doubt satisfactory, as Singapore decided to invest in additional Skyhawks several years later. On this occasion though, the entire remanufacture project was to be undertaken in-country and no fewer than 86 redundant Navy machines were shipped to Singapore in the early 1980s. The majority—70 aircraft—were A-4Cs, transfer being accomplished during 1980. These were followed by 16 TA-4Bs in 1983. Thus far, Singapore has not made public the full extent of this programme but it is generally accepted that around 40 single-seat A-4S-1s and eight two-seat TA-4S-1s will be completed and the first of the former was actually rolled out as long ago as February 1982. Delivery of these aircraft to No.145 Squadron duly began later that year and it seems likely that a fourth Skyhawk unit will eventually form.

Looking ahead a few years, future investment in the Skyhawk—or Skywarrior as it is rather confusingly known by the Singaporeans—should result in a marked increase in overall capability, with presently in hand update programmes likely to boost performance and accuracy of weapons delivery. Dealing with the former aspect first, substitution of an unreheated General Electric F404 engine for the existing Wright J65 should result in payload and range benefits but this project is apparently running late, for the first of two planned prototypes had yet to fly at time of making, despite the fact that the maiden flight was targeted for 1986.

Delays have definitely occurred on the avionics front, the initial proposal to incorporate a Lear-Siegler package being blocked by the US government which was not prepared to sanction the technology transfer. In consequence, Singapore has turned to Britain in its endeavours to improve Skyhawk capability in this area. Ferranti's Type 4510 head-up display unit and Litton's LN-39 Intertial

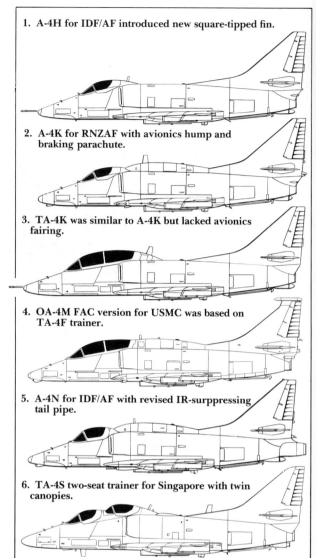

1. A-4H for IDF/AF introduced new square-tipped fin.

2. A-4K for RNZAF with avionics hump and braking parachute.

3. TA-4K was similar to A-4K but lacked avionics fairing.

4. OA-4M FAC version for USMC was based on TA-4F trainer.

5. A-4N for IDF/AF with revised IR-surppressing tail pipe.

6. TA-4S two-seat trainer for Singapore with twin canopies.

Nav-Attack System are just two elements of a much revamped avionics suite which it seems will be retrospectively installed in at least 40 aircraft.

If Singapore's interest in the A-4 remains high, the same cannot be said of Kuwait, which has apparently put its Skyhawks up for sale, even though they were amongst the last to be built. Placed in late 1974, the contract covered 30 A-4KU single-seaters (first flight 20 July 1976) and half-a-dozen TA-4KU trainers (first flight 14 December 1976) which were eventually delivered via the United Kingdom in 1977-78.

Since procurement was accomplished via US Navy channels, Navy bureau numbers were allocated, the A-4KUs employing serial numbers in the 160180-160209 block while the TA-4KUs used 160210-160215. These were retained until the aircraft

actually reached Kuwait, US national insignia also being applied for test and ferry flying. On arrival in Kuwait, the A-4KUs acquired new identities in the range 801-830 and the TA-4KUs became 881-886.

Intended to provide a measure of strike capability against neighbouring Iraq, these Skyhawks served with two KAF squadrons before the 35 survivors were withdrawn from use at Ahmad al Jabar air base during 1984. In the intervening period, a commendably low attrition rate had been experienced, just one A-4KU having been lost in five years of service. However, it is possible that utilisation was also low.

Seventh nation

Destined to be the seventh overseas nation to acquire Skyhawks, Indonesia received an initial batch of 14 A-4Es and two TA-4Hs from Israel in 1980, following up with a second identical group from the same source in 1985. In *Tentara Nasional Indonesia - Angkatan Udara* (TNI-AU, Indonesian National Armed Force - Air Force) service, these are distributed between two squadrons, namely No.11 at Madiun and No.12 at Pakenbaru.

Last, but by no means least, Malaysia joined the ranks of Skyhawk operators in late 1984 when the first examples of an eventual total of 40 aircraft were delivered, following extensive refurbishment by Grumman. In fact, the 34 A-4PTMs and six

Above: Displaying the national insignia of Malaysia, this TA-4PTM was the first of six to be delivered, a further 34 single-seaters finding their way into service after remanufacture by Grumman.

TA-4PTMs (Peculiar to Malaysia) that eventually found their way into *Tentara Udara Diraja Malaysia* (TUDM) service were the survivors of no less than 25 A-4Cs and 63 A-4Ls that were removed from storage in the early 1980s and shipped to Grumman's St Augustine facility in Florida where conversion work was accomplished.

Cost considerations meant that renovation was less ambitious than at first proposed and the resulting aircraft are by no means to a common standard, one instance of this being provided by the fact that only about half are compatible with the AGM-65 Maverick air-to-surface missile. Equipment common to all includes the Hughes Aircraft Angle Rate Bombing System (ARBS) incorporating a laser seeker head and, in theory, permitting precise delivery of laser-guided weaponry. Wiring for the AIM-9 Sidewinder is also installed throughout Malaysia's Skyhawk fleet.

Delivery of the 40 aircraft destined to join TUDM was accomplished between the end of 1984 and January 1986, TA-4PTMs being allocated serial numbers in the sequence M32-01 to M32-06 while the A-4PTMs ran from M32-07 to M32-40. These are now fully operational from Kuantan air base, with No.6 "Naga" Squadron, which introduced the type to service during 1985. A second unit – No.9 "Jebat" Squadron—formed on Skyhawks in 1986.

5

The Skyhawk in Combat

FLYING FOR the first time just months after the Korean War ended in stalemate, the Skyhawk had to wait several years before it was eventually employed in the role for which it was designed. Although it came close to seeing combat on a number of occasions during the next few years—most notably in summer 1958 when A4D-2s of VA-83 covered the Marine landing near Beirut and again in the early 1960s at the time of the "Bay of Pigs" debacle in Cuba—it was not until August 1964 that it finally released its first load of bombs in anger. Since then, it would probably be accurate to say that scarcely a year has passed without the A-4 being in action somewhere, aircraft from Israel and Argentina following their US counterparts into combat and, in turn, making a significant contribution to the Skyhawk legend.

The first Vietnam strike mission arose in response to the Gulf of Tonkin incident of 2 August 1964 and took the form of a reprisal raid against North Vietnamese motor torpedo boat bases. Staged on 5 August, by carrier-borne aircraft of the 7th Fleet operating from the USS *Constellation* and the USS *Ticonderoga*, some 64 sorties were eventually completed under operation "Pierce Arrow". These apparently resulted in about two dozen MTBs being destroyed or seriously damaged. At the same time, support facilities used by the MTBs were thoroughly worked over, fuel dumps being hard hit in a series of attacks by A-4C Skyhawks from *Constellation's* Carrier Air Wing 14 (VA-144 and VA-146 squadrons) as well as A-4Es from VA-55 and VA-56 on the *Ticonderoga* with Carrier Air Wing Five (CVW-5).

As it transpired, "Pierce Arrow" proved to be merely an overture for what followed but it was not until early 1965 that the A-4 again hit the headlines by participating in a major air raid against North Vietnam. Once again, the object was retaliatory, aircraft from the *Ranger, Coral Sea* and *Hancock* hitting back after Viet Cong guerillas succeeded in causing a considerable amount of damage and quite a few casualties in a number of attacks on US facilities in and around Pleiku.

On this occasion, reprisal was prompt, the go-ahead for "Flaming Dart I" coming within hours of the Viet Cong raids. Indeed, Navy aircraft were in action on the same afternoon, with A-4C and A-4E Skyhawks from VA-93, VA-94, VA-153, VA-155, VA-212 and VA-216 almost certainly all being involved in a major raid on military barracks near Dong Hoi in southern North Vietnam.

Swift and deadly

Almost inevitably, this generated a swift and deadly Viet Cong response near Qui Nhon, where 30 US and Vietnamese servicemen were killed on 10 February. Staying true to the "tit-for-tat" policy, "Flaming Dart II' was quickly organised, being perhaps even more ambitious in that it involved elements of the USAF, USN and VNAF in co-ordinated attacks on military installations at Chanh Hoa and Vit Thu Lu. Once again, the A-4 was committed to combat but events then quietened down before, on 26 March 1965, Navy pilots were again despatched to North Vietnam. This time, however, the attack was the harbinger for the sustained aerial bombardment which soon became better known as "Rolling Thunder" and which had, as its primary objective, the systematic destruction of the North's capacity to wage war.

In the event "Rolling Thunder" failed to achieve this goal but that failure cannot be attributed to the airmen who did all that was asked of them and more before many of them became disillusioned by Washington's handling of the campaign. All that lay in the future, however, when aircraft launched from the *Coral Sea* and the *Hancock* for "Rolling Thunder I", their targets being key radar sites in the vicinity of Vinh Son.

At that time, although the A-4B did still equip a few front line squadrons, it was being supplanted by the much improved A-4E variant. In view of that, it was hardly surprising that the A-4E and A-4C shared responsibility for carrying the war to North Vietnam during the first few years of conflict. Eventually, of course, the A-4F also played a significant part, this derivative being introduced to combat by VA-23 and VA-192 in January 1968.

The only other Skyhawk model to see action was the rather older A-4B which eventually made it to the war zone in 1966 when VA-15 and VA-95 operated from the USS *Intrepid*. Having earlier been reclassified as an anti-submarine warfare carrier (CVS), this vessel rather unusually embarked an Air Wing (CVW-10) made up entirely of light and medium attack squadrons with A-4B Skyhawks and A-1H/J Skyraiders.

Below: An A-4C Skyhawk from VA-146 aboard the USS *Constellation* pulls off target after releasing another load of ordnance during an attack on Army barracks at Hai Dong, North Vietnam in October 1967.

Above: Pictured aboard the USS *Hancock* during that carrier's 1967 WestPac combat cruise, two bomb-laden A-4E Skyhawks of VA-93 are readied for launch on another strike against North Vietnam.

Returning to combat in 1967, *Intrepid* again included the A-4B in its complement, this time from a near-unique unit in the shape of Anti-Submarine Fighter Squadron Three (VSF-3). This was one of just two squadrons – the other was VSF-1—which formed in the 1960s to provide ASW aircraft carriers with some defensive capability, the idea being to allocate small detachments to the various Anti-Submarine Warfare Carrier Air Groups (CVSGs).

As far as 7th Fleet operations were concerned, the carriers engaged in support of the war effort invariably cruised the waters of the Tonkin Gulf or the South China Sea. From the former location, they could launch and recover aircraft in relative safety since the likelihood of North Vietnam's Air Force or Navy attempting to interfere was so remote as to be virtually dismissed. In addition, during the early phase of escalation—between 20 May 1965 and 4 August 1966—the Navy furnished some tactical air power over South Vietnam and this was satisfied by carriers positioned in the South China Sea. In order to identify the different operating areas, these were known as "stations".

That in the south was referred to as "Dixie Station", Task Force 77 generally assigning one carrier to this location, with aircraft being employed against targets in the south. Since this provided an excellent opportunity for aircrews to get used to combat in an area of low-risk, it was usual for each carrier to spend a few days at "Dixie" at the start of each line period before moving north to "Yankee Station" in Tonkin Gulf. There, of course, targets were almost always heavily defended and operations from "Yankee Station" were seldom unopposed.

Eventually, following the massive increase in USAF resources in South Vietnam, in-country tactical air requirements could at last be adequately met and operations from "Dixie" ceased in August 1966, carriers assigned to the 7th Fleet thereafter working only from "Yankee Station". Targets generally lay in the four "route package" areas of North Vietnam that were assigned to the Navy.

Basically intended to ensure the best use of available air power, the Route Package concept was hammered out by the joint 2nd Air Division/Task Force 77 "Rolling Thunder" Co-ordinating Committee in the spring of 1965 and effectively divided North Vietnam into several clearly-defined geographical areas.

Route Package I extended north from the demilitarised zone to a point just above the 18th parallel and was essentially assigned to the USAF, strikes in this area being undertaken at the direction of the Military Assistance Command Vietnam (MACV). Route Package II came next and was under control of TF-77, this covering the area from the 18th parallel to just below the 19th parallel and including Vinh.

TF-77 also exercised control over Route Packages III and IV. Bounded to the south by RPII and to the east by the Laotian border, RPIII contained few significant targets although Route 7 and the Barthelemy Pass were the subject of near constant interdiction, supplies destined for Pathet Lao and North Vietnamese forces on the Plain of Jars passing through this key "choke-point". Immediately to the north, RPIV included the celebrated Thanh Hoa bridge, the major logistics centre at Nam Dinh and an extensive rail and road network.

"No-go" area

Route Package V was entrusted to the Air Force and was by far the largest single area. Extending westwards from the 105 degree 30 minute line of longitude, it was bounded to the south by an imaginary extension of the north-east rail line to a point of intersection with the Laotian border. To the north lay China—quite definitely a "no-go" area—while to the west was Laos, ostensibly neutral territory.

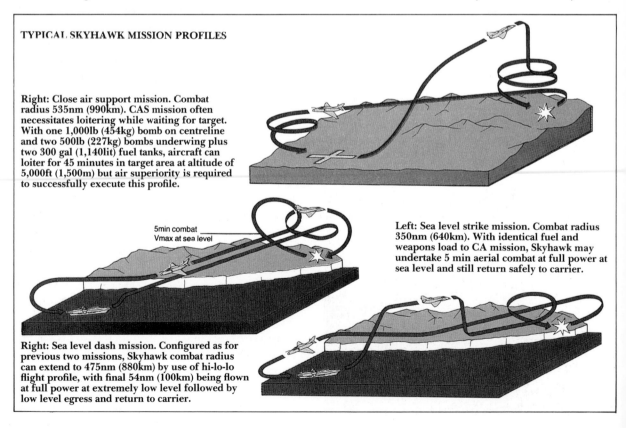

TYPICAL SKYHAWK MISSION PROFILES

Right: Close air support mission. Combat radius 535nm (990km). CAS mission often necessitates loitering while waiting for target. With one 1,000lb (454kg) bomb on centreline and two 500lb (227kg) bombs underwing plus two 300 gal (1,140lit) fuel tanks, aircraft can loiter for 45 minutes in target area at altitude of 5,000ft (1,500m) but air superiority is required to successfully execute this profile.

5min combat
Vmax at sea level

Left: Sea level strike mission. Combat radius 350nm (640km). With identical fuel and weapons load to CA mission, Skyhawk may undertake 5 min aerial combat at full power at sea level and still return safely to carrier.

Right: Sea level dash mission. Configured as for previous two missions, Skyhawk combat radius can extend to 475nm (880km) by use of hi-lo-lo flight profile, with final 54nm (100km) being flown at full power at extremely low level followed by low level egress and return to carrier.

Finally, there was the dreaded Route Package VI which embraced that part of North Vietnam to the east of the 105 degree 30 minute line of longitude, the southernmost boundary being an imaginary line just to the north of Nam Dinh. With by far the greatest concentration of targets—and, not surprisingly, the strongest defences—RPVI was further divided into two portions along the north-east railway line, 7th Air Force controlling RPVIA to the west while TF-77 managed RPVIB to the east.

Major objectives included the military industrial complexes of Hanoi and Haiphong, the Doumer bridge and the Thai Nguyen, Kinh Nho and Kep railroad yards as well as airfields at Hoa Lac, Kep and Phuc Yen. However, since many targets lay close together, the North Vietnamese were able to compress their defences, a formidable array of around 2,000 37-mm and 57-mm anti-aircraft artillery (AAA) pieces being present in RPVI during 1967-68. Further "threats" included about 800 85-mm and 100-mm guns plus the SA-2 Guideline surface-to-air missile (SAM).

Inevitably, these took their toll of Navy aircraft

Above: Strike camera's eye view of a raid on a petroleum storage site at My Xa, North Vietnam on 19 July 1967. A-4Cs of VA-76 and A-4Es of VA-212 on the USS _Bon Homme Richard_ were involved.

although the price paid was perhaps not as high as that of the USAF which was less fortunate in that operations from bases in Thailand often dictated "running the gauntlet" of more than 100 miles of heavily defended airspace. Navy pilots, on the other hand, seldom had to penetrate more than 25 miles from the coast to reach their targets—once there, of course, they generally faced the same degree of risk, Thanh Hoa, Vinh and Haiphong all possessing defensive networks which approached those of Hanoi in terms of the intensity of firepower.

As far as the Navy's Skyhawk-equipped light attack squadrons (VAs) are concerned, most eventually took this type into combat during the period from 1964 to 1973. A-4s of various sub-types served with no less than 42 VA units, six of which were non-combatant, being concerned solely with the task of training. For the record, VA-43, VA-44 and VA-45 fulfilled this function with the Atlantic Fleet Naval Air Force (NavAirLant) while VA-125, VA-126 and VA-127 satisfied NavAirPac requirements in this area.

Thus, some 36 squadrons ultimately employed the type in a front-line capacity but rather than list those squadrons which did use the Skyhawk in combat, it is easier to provide details of the five which did not.

Two of them—VA-133 and VA-134—were destined to enjoy only a brief period of existence, for little more than a year from August 1961, but all of the other three—VA-64, VA-81 and VA-83—were

Below: A deck edge catapult operator on USS _Intrepid_ "tensions" an A-4C of VA-66 in anticipation of launch during the course of combat operations in the Gulf of Tonkin in September 1968.

equipped with the Skyhawk throughout the 1960s, a decade in which they completed several cruises in Atlantic and Mediterranean waters but never made it to WestPac. As it turned out, VA-64 was deactivated at the beginning of 1970 while VA-81 and VA-83 both progressed to the A-7E Corsair II in that same year.

Operations against the North were at first targeted on lines of communication (LOC), key "choke" points like railroad yards, bridges and river crossings which were repeatedly struck in the effort to strangle the flow of supplies. As the Navy's primary light attack type, the Skyhawk carried the burden more or less single-handedly until the rather more capable A-7 Corsair II began to reach Fleet units in 1968. In view of that it was hardly surprising that attrition was high, many A-4s falling foul of North Vietnamese defences between 1965 and 1968.

What began in optimism progressively degenerated into disillusionment when it became evident that the North Vietnamese were extremely skilled at improvising repairs and, perhaps of even greater significance, at disguising their handiwork. This had the result of rendering much of the on-going reconnaissance more or less valueless for many of the targets which were thought to have been put out of action did in fact remain in nightly use. In consequence, it was always difficult to effectively interdict the North's capacity to wage war, Navy objectives gradually taking the form of what could be described

Above: With empty multiple ejection racks on the inner wingstore stations and an auxiliary fuel tank on the centreline, an A-4E of VMA-223 "Bulldogs" returns to Chu Lai at the end of a mission.

as more a campaign of harassment, repeated attacks on LOCs disrupting but never entirely stopping the movement of men and material.

With attacks on LOCs failing to achieve the desired result, attention was then turned to the industrial base, it being felt that the destruction of North Vietnam's manufacturing capability would lead to peace. On the contrary, North Vietnamese ingenuity soon rendered this idea null and void, this phase of the campaign achieving little more than forcing dispersal of light and heavy industry. While the bombing may have been inconvenient for the North, it merely seems to have succeeded in stiffening resolve.

Point the finger

With the benefit of hindsight, it is easy to point the finger at those in Washington as the architects of America's failure to defeat North Vietnam; the piecemeal application of air power between 1965 and 1968 and the periodic bombing halts of the "Rolling Thunder" era permitting those in the North to gradually adjust in response to changing circumstances. In truth, it is doubtful if even wholesale, indiscriminate bombing would have succeeded for, in the final analysis, the South Vietnamese evidently lacked the will of their counterparts in the north. Thus, while mass bombing might have brought about a temporary ceasefire at a much earlier date, it seems unlikely that it would have resulted in enduring peace.

For its part in the air war, a typical Skyhawk payload would have been around 2,500lb (1,134kg) of ordnance. Conventional "iron" bombs of the Mk.81 250lb (113kg) and Mk.82 500lb (226kg) low-drag "Snakeye" types were widely used while Maxson's AGM-12 Bullpup air-to-surface missile was another weapon which was particularly common, especially during the early phases of "Rolling Thunder". Unguided Zumi rockets also featured, being used against "soft" coastal shipping. Another missile that found favour was the AGM-45 Shrike, A-4s employed in "Wild Weasel"-type SAM-suppression utilising this anti-radiation weapon to good effect against the radar control equipment associated with the SA-2 Guideline. Heavier bombs were also used against "hard" targets, these being epitomised by the 2,000lb (907kg) Mk.84. And, of course, there was also the integral 20-mm cannon armament which was a handy "tool" for strafing in situations where the threat from ground defences was considered low.

Below: A deck crew earns its pay the hard way as it positons an A-4E of VA-106 on one of Intrepid's catapults in September 1968. Note that this Skyhawk has acquired a dorsal avionics "hump".

Moving from the Navy to the Marine Corps, this service was slower to commit its Skyhawks to action, and neither was quite such a high proportion of its resources called upon to perform close air support in Vietnam. Nevertheless, in just under eight years of war, seven of the 11 USMC attack squadrons (VMA) which were using the Skyhawk at the start of 1965 did complete at least one tour in Vietnam and a few were present for prolonged periods.

Although the first USMC combat aircraft reached South Vietnam in early 1965, it was not until the summer of that year that the Skyhawk was called upon to perform an active role, deployment coinciding with the opening of a new base at Chu Lai. Work on construction began in May 1965 and was carried though with such haste that the new base was able to open for business on 1 June, although facilities were somewhat spartan.

Initially, air operations required use of the SATS (short airfield for tactical support) concept, a 3,600-foot ((1,079m) strip being provided. Subsequently, a 10,000-foot (3,048m)) paved runway was brought into commission but early operations were dependent on use of catapults, JATO (jet-assisted take-off) augmentation and arrester gear. Initial occupants of Chu Lai comprised the A-4Cs of VMA-225 and the A-4Es of VMA-311, both units taking up residence on 1 June and performing their first combat missions later that day.

Skyhawks stationed at Chu Lai came under the control of Marine Aircraft Group 12 (MAG-12) which added a third squadron later in June when the A-4Cs of VMA-214 arrived from Kaneohe Bay, Hawaii. The number of aircraft rose to even higher levels in mid-October with the appearance of VMA-211's A-4Es. Since each squadron had a unit establishment of about 20 Skyhawks, MAG-12 at Chu Lai now exercised control over a fleet of some 80 aircraft, a level which fluctuated slightly during the next couple of years as units rotated in and out, VMA-224 relieving VMA-225 in October 1965 and VMA-311 giving way to VMA-223 in December.

For the most part, such rotations were confined to squadron personnel, the Skyhawks already in place at Chu Lai being "inherited" by the incoming unit. Thus, during the first two years of operations, seven squadrons were committed to combat, these comprising VMA-121 which arrived in December 1966; VMA-211 (October 1965 until July 1966 and again from October 1966); VMA-214 (June 1965 to February 1966 and May 1966 to March 1967); VMA-223 (December 1965 to December 1966 and from March 1967); VMA-224 (October 1965 to April 1966 and July to November 1966); VMA-225 (June to October 1965) and VMA-311 (June to December 1965 and from February 1966).

Thereafter, the situation settled down with the result that from summer 1967 until base closure in July 1970, there were never less than three and no more than four squadrons in residence at any time. Units which shared the responsibility for providing close air support throughout this period comprised VMA-121, VMA-211, VMA-223 and VMA-311.

All four were certainly present in January 1969, VMA-121 flying the A-4C variant while the other three squadrons all used the later A-4E but VMA-121 had returned to the USA to convert to the A-6A Intruder by the summer. As far as the other three squadrons were concerned, these soldiered on with MAG-12 until 1970 when reductions of US forces in Vietnam drastically curtailed Marine combat operations with the A-4.

First to leave was VMA-223, 20 A-4Es accompanying 15 F-4B Phantoms of VMFA-542 in the largest trans-Pacific ferry flight to be undertaken by USMC aircraft thus far. Given the code-name "Key Wallop", the 8,000-mile (12,875km) journey began on 28 January and culminated in a safe return to El Toro, California on 8 February, intermediate stops being made at Cubi Point in the Philippines, at Wake Island and Hawaii.

Even as VMA-223 was settling in at El Toro, further action was being taken to reduce combat forces at Chu Lai, VMA-211 and MAG-12 moving out to Iwakuni, Japan on 12 February. For the first time, just one USMC A-4 squadron was present in South Vietnam VMA-311 held this distinction and the departure of MAG-12 meant that the "Tomcats" now reported to a new "parent", namely MAG-12, also at Chu Lai.

For VMA-311, though, life continued much as before until the summer when it shifted quarters to Da Nang. This transfer was accompanied by reassignment to MAG-11 which continued to exercise control for another nine months, the squadron flying its 47,663rd and last combat sortie on 7 May 1971. Five days later, VMA-311 took 21 A-4Es to Iwakuni and, for the USMC Skyhawk squadrons, it looked as though the war was over, the "Tomcats" feeling particularly aggrieved at failing to complete 50,000 combat sorties.

As it turned out, they did pass this milestone, VMA-311 being part of the US response to the North Vietnamese offensive of spring 1972. Alerted to prepare for a hasty movement on 12 May, the squadron was back in Vietnam five days later, this time at Bien Hoa, a few miles to the north-east of Saigon. Once again, the parent group was MAG-12 which also exercised control over a second A-4 squadron, namely VMA-211.

Led by the particularly appropriately named Colonel Dean C. Macho, MAG-12 aircraft flew their first sorties on the 19th, striking targets in the southern half of South Vietnam. Such was the pace of activity that it didn't take VMA-311 long to reach the elusive 50,000 sortie mark, this milestone being passed on 29 August. By the time of the 27 January 1973 ceasefire, a further 4,625 combat sorties had been recorded but with the war now over VMA-311 wasted little time in redeploying to Iwakuni, departing from Bien Hoa for the last time on the 29th.

Close air support

In Vietnam, USMC Skyhawks were principally concerned with close air support, operating in conjunction with Marine ground troops of the 1st and 3rd Marine Divisions in the I Corps area as well as those of the US Army and ARVN. In addition, some interdiction missions were flown, generally involving targets in Laos, Cambodia and Route Package I.

Ordnance loads varied according to circumstance, with bombs, napalm and rockets all being used while the Skyhawk's somewhat limited integral gun armament was augmented by the Hughes Mk.4 gun pod. It was possible for two such pods to be carried, complete with about 1,300 rounds of 20-mm ammunition.

The latter weapon was particularly useful when called upon to escort Marine helicopters, cells of two A-4s generally working in conjunction with

Above: A brace of A-4E Skyhawks from USMC attack squadron VMA-311 take a drink from a KC-130F Hercules of VMGR-152 during January 1971 when the 'Tomcats" were based at Da Nang with MAG-11.

UH-1E gunships to protect unarmed or lightly-armed "slicks" (troop-carrying helicopters). By flying the so-called "daisy chain" pattern, the Skyhawk escorts were usually able to remain within three miles of the "slicks" and were thus able to respond quickly to requests for fire support. A closely allied mission would require A-4s, F-4 Phantoms or F-8 Crusaders to "work over" the LZ (landing zone) in advance of the helicopters' arrival.

In more conventional bombing operations, widespread use was made of the General Electric TPQ-10 radar control system which permitted combat operations to be accomplished with a fair measure of success in poor weather or by night. Bascially, the TPQ-10 radar was used to track and control Marine Corps strike aircraft, ground-based air support radar teams guiding strike formations to the target area and advising pilots when to release their ordnance. Use of TPQ-10 quickly expanded to encompass virtually the entire I Corps tactical zone and some idea of the dependence on this system can be gained from the fact that 31 per cent of the combat sorties (4,993 to be precise) flown by USMC aircraft in the last quarter of 1966 involved radar controlled weapons release procedures.

As far as Marine Skyhawk operations are concerned, although it was the VMA units which bore the heaviest load, no review of combat activity would be complete without brief mention of the part played by the Headquarters and Maintenance Squadrons (H&MS). Assigned directly to the MAGs (and, incidentally, sharing the same number), three such squadrons are known to have utilised two-seat Skyhawks in Vietnam, these being employed on forward air control and visual reconnaissance tasks.

Replacing the veteran TF-9J Cougar from late 1967, the TA-4F eventually operated with H&MS-12 and H&MS-13 from Chu Lai and with H&MS-11 from Da Nang but it is doubtful if the three squadrons ever possessed more than ten aircraft between them. Smoke rockets were employed for target marking and the TA-4F also boasted limited strike capability, being able to use unguided air-to-ground rockets against "soft" targets.

Other battle fronts

As far as Israeli use of the Skyhawk in combat is concerned, relatively little is known despite the fact that it has been in the thick of the action for many years. Attaining operational status early in 1968, the A-4H was soon in action in a series of raids on terrorist camps on the east bank of the River Jordan and it soon demonstrated that it was no slouch when it came to "mixing it" in aerial combat, IDF/AF Skyhawks downing Syrian MiG-17s and MiG-19s on a number of occasions.

In 1973, the A-4 was also in the forefront at a time when the IDF/AF's much-trumpeted superiority came under serious threat, some reports indicating that around 50 Skyhawks were destroyed by anti-aircraft artillery or surface-to-air missiles of either the radar-guided or heat-seeking type. That the latter weapon was particularly successful would appear to be borne out by the fact that Israel subsequently initiated a quite extensive modification programme aimed at reducing the aircraft's obviously troublesome infra-red signature. This eventually culminated in most Israeli Skyhawks acquiring a much-extended tail pipe which seems to have been successful.

If Israel's combat use of the Skyhawk has been the subject of official reticence, the same cannot be said of Argentina, this type's contribution to the 1982 Falklands conflict being particularly well documented. Space limitations unfortunately permit little more than a cursory look at Argentinian use of the Skyhawk but both the Air Force and the Navy achieved a fair measure of success in the brief but often bloody war, during which they operated entirely from shore bases, in-flight refuelling often being a vital adjunct in the successful execution of an attack.

From Argentina's viewpoint, the destruction of two British warships—HMS *Coventry* and HMS

Above: Although it lacks squadron insignia, this A-4E was from VA-23 aboard the USS *Midway*. It is seen delivering a load of 250-lb bombs on a Viet Cong enclave in South Vietnam in October 1965.

Ardent—was undoubtedly the high point of the air war but the A-4s also inflicted extensive damage on HMS *Argonaut*, HMS *Broadsword* and HMS *Glasgow*. Other successes include the destruction of RFA *Sir Galahad* at Port Pleasant in an attack which also seriously damaged RFA *Sir Tristram* and resulted in 51 British soldiers being killed and a further 46 being injured, many seriously.

Below: Bomb runners wheel fresh ordnance across the flight deck of the *Bon Homme Richard* towards A-4E Skyhawks of VA-94 in 1968. Sister squadrons VA-93 and VA-212 operated the later A-4F model.

Such achievements were not accomplished without loss, however, and of the 50 or so A-4B/Ps, A-4Cs and A-4Qs available at the start of the conflict, no fewer than 22 failed to return in the course of executing 289 combat sorties. Not all fell victim to the British defences. Two succumbed to the elements while another was shot down by Argentinian gunners at Goose Green after successfully attacking HMS *Glasgow* and forcing that vessel's early return to the United Kingdom.

The other 19 were all destroyed by the British, eight by AIM-9L Sidewinders fired by Sea Harriers and the rest to a mixture of ground or sea-based defences including Sea Wolf and Sea Dart surface-to-air missiles and anti-aircraft artillery. As if that wasn't bad enough, the survivors eventually learned that many of the bombs they battled so hard to deliver had failed to detonate, as they were dropped from too low an altitude for correct arming. Had pilots been alerted to this problem earlier, it is conceivable that British losses would have been much heavier.

APPENDIX I: A-4 Skyhawk Production

Variant	Bu.Nos.	Quantity
XA-4A	137812	1
A-4A	137813-137831	19
A-4A	139919-139970	52
A-4B	142082-142141	60
A-4A	142142-142235	94
A-4B	142416-142423	8
A-4B	142674-142953	280
A-4B	144868-145061	194
A-4C	145062-145146	85
A-4C	147669-147849	181
A-4C	148304-148317	14
A-4C	148435-148612	178
A-4E	148613-148614	2
A-4C	149487-149646	160
A-4E	149647-149666	20
A-4E	149959-150138	180
A-4C	150581-150600	20
A-4E	151022-151201	180
A-4E	151984-152100	117
A-4F	152101	1
TA-4E	152102-152103	2
TA-4F	152846-152878	33
TA-4F	153459-153531	73
TA-4F	153660-153690	31
A-4F	154172-154217	46
TA-4F	154287-154343	57
TA-4F	154614-154657	44
A-4G	154903-154910	8
TA-4G	154911-154912	2
A-4F	154970-155069	100
TA-4J	155070	1
TA-4F	155071	1
TA-4J	155072-155119	48
A-4H	155242-155289	48
TA-4J	156891-156950	60
A-4H	157395-157428	34
TA-4H	157429-157434	6
A-4K	157904-157913	10
TA-4K	157914-157917	4
A-4H	157918-157925	8
TA-4H	157926-157929	4
TA-4J	158073-158147	75
A-4M	158148-158196	49
A-4M	158412-158435	24
TA-4J	158453-158527	75
TA-4J	158712-158723	12
A-4N	158726-158743	18
A-4N	159035-159052	18
A-4N	159075-159098	24
TA-4J	159099-159104	6
A-4M	159470-159493	24
A-4N	159515-159545	31
TA-4J	159546-159556	11

Above: Douglas engineers employ a small crane and a certain amount of muscle power as they tackle the task of changing a Wright J65 engine on an early production Skyhawk at El Segundo.

A-4M	159778-159790	13
TA-4J	159795-159798	4
A-4N	159799-159824	26
A-4M	160022-160045	24
A-4KU	160180-160209	30
TA-4KU	160210-160215	6
A-4M	160241-160264	24
	Total production	**2,960**

APPENDIX II: CURRENT OPERATORS

US Navy
VA-127, Lemoore, California—A-4F, TA-4J
VAQ-33, Key West, Florida—EA-4F, TA-4J
VC-1, Barbers Point, Hawaii—TA-4J
VC-5, Cubi Point, Philippines—TA-4J
VC-8, Roosevelt Roads, Puerto Rico—TA-4J
VC-10, Guantanamo Bay, Cuba—TA-4J
VC-12*, Oceana, Virginia—A-4F, TA-4J
VC-13*, Miramar, California—TA-4J
VF-43, Oceana, Virginia—A-4E/F, TA-4J
VF-45, Key West, Florida—A-4E, TA-4J
VF-126, Miramar, California—A-4F, TA-4J
VT-7, Meridian, Mississippi—TA-4J
VT-21, Kingsville, Texas—TA-4J

continued over

VT-22, Kingsville, Texas—TA-4J
VT-24, Chase Field, Texas—TA-4J
VT-25, Chase Field, Texas—TA-4J
VT-86, Pensacola, Florida—TA-4J
VX-4, Point Mugu, California—TA-4J
VX-5, China Lake, California—A-4M, TA-4J
Fighter Weapons School, Miramar, California—TA-4J
Naval Air Engineering Center, Lakehurst, New Jersey—NTA-4F
Naval Air Reserve Unit*, Dallas, Texas—TA-4J
Naval Air Test Center, Patuxent River, Maryland—A-4M, TA-4J
Naval Test Pilots School, Patuxent River, Mayland—TA-4J
Naval Weapons Center, China Lake, California—A-4M

US Marine Corps
H&MS-12, Iwakuni, Japan—OA-4M
H&MS-13, El Toro, California—OA-4M
H&MS-24, Kaneohe Bay, Hawaii—TA-4F
H&MS-31, Beaufort, South Carolina—TA-4F
H&MS-32, Cherry Point, North Carolina—OA-4M
H&MS-42*, Alameda, California—TA-4J
H&MS-49*, Willow Grove, Pennsylvania—TA-4J
VMA-124*, Memphis, Tennessee—A-4E, TA-4J
VMA-131*, Willow Grove, Pennsylvania—A-4E
VMA-133*, Alameda, California—A-4F, TA-4J
VMA-142*, Cecil Field, Florida—A-4F
VMA-211, El Toro, California—A-4M
VMA-214, El Toro, California—A-4M
VMA-223, Cherry Point, North Carolina—A-4M
VMA-311, El Toro, California—A-4M
VMA-322*, South Weymouth, Massachusetts—A-4M
VMAT-102, Yuma, Arizona—A-4M, TA-4F

Key: H&MS - Headquarters and Maintenance Squadron; VA - Attack Squadron; VAQ - Tactical Electronic Warfare Squadron; VC - Composite Squadron; VF - Fighter Squadron; VMA - Marine Attack Squadron; VMAT - Marine Attack Training Squadron; VT - Training Squadron; VX - Air Test and Evaluation Squadron, * - Reserve unit.

OVERSEAS AIR ARMS
Argentina - Air Force
Grupo 4 de Caza (Bombardeo), Los Tamarindos, Mendoza
III Escuadrone de Caza Bombardeo - A-4C
Grupo 5 de Caza (Bombardeo), Villa Reynolds, San Luis
IV Escuadrone de Caza Bombardeo - A-4B/P
 V Escuadrone de Caza Bombardeo - A-4B/P

Argentina - Navy
3 Esc de Caza y Ataque, Comandante Espora, Buenos Aires - A-4Q

Indonesia
Skwadron Udara 11, Madiun - A-4E/TA/4H
Skwadron Udara 12, Pakenbaru - A-4E/TA-4H

Israel
No details known with regard to unit identities. Still reported to be operating survivors of A-4E/H/N and TA-4H/J with four squadrons at Eqron Air Base and other locations.

Kuwait
Aircraft apparently not operational, being held in storage at Ahmad al Jabar Air Base since 1984 pending sale.

Malaysia
No.6 "Naga" Squadron, Kuantan - A-4PTM/TA-4PTM
No.9 "Jebat" Squadron, Kuantan - A-4PTM/TA-4PTM

New Zealand
No.2 Squadron, Ohakea - A-4G/TA-4G
No.75 Squadron, Ohakea - A-4K/TA-4K

Singapore
No.142 "Gryphon" Squadron, Tengah - A-4S/TA-4S
No.143 "Phoenix" Squadron, Tengah - A-4S/TA-4S
No.145 Squadron, Tengah - A-4S-1/TA-4S-1

Below: Taken during carrier qualification and shakedown trials in the Caribbean in April 1965, this photograph shows a VA-64 A-4C being readied for launch from the newly-commissioned USS *America*.

APPENDIX III: Modification Programmes

TA-4B   Unknown number of modifications for service with second-line elements of USN/USMC Reserve Force.

EA-4F   Four TA-4F modified for ECM "aggressor" role. Aircraft involved are: 152852, 152869, 153481 and 154655.

A-4L   100 A-4C aircraft modified for USN/USMC use. Serial numbers are: 145065, 145076, 145077, 145078, 145092, 145101, 145103, 145114, 145117, 145119, 145121, 145122, 145128, 145133, 145141, 147669, 147671, 147690, 147703, 147706, 147708, 147717, 147723, 147727, 147736, 147750, 147754, 147761, 147768, 147772, 147780, 147782, 147787, 147793, 147796, 147798, 147802, 147807, 147815, 147825, 147827, 147836, 147843, 148306, 148307, 148316, 148436, 148446, 148453, 148479, 148487, 148490, 148498, 148505, 148530, 148538, 148555, 148578, 148581, 148586, 148588, 148600, 148602, 148611, 149497, 149500, 149502, 149506, 149508, 149516, 149518, 149531, 149532, 149536, 149539, 149540, 149551, 149555, 149556, 149569, 149573, 149579, 149583, 149591, 149593, 149595, 149604, 149607, 149608, 149620, 149623, 149626, 149630, 149633, 149635, 149640, 149646, 150586, 150593, 150598.

OA-4M   23 TA-4F modified to this configuration for service with USMC H&MS units in forward air control task. Identities comprise: 152856, 152874, 153507, 153510, 153527, 153529, 153531, 154294, 154306, 154307, 154328, 154333, 154335, 154336, 154340, 154623, 154624, 154628, 154630, 154633, 154638, 154645 and 154651.

A-4P   50 A-4B aircraft modified for service with the Fuerza Aerea Argentina. Are referred to locally as A-4Bs. No previous identities are known.

A-4PTM   88 A-4C/L aircraft acquired for Malaysia. Delivery of resulting 34 A-4PTMs and six TA-4PTMs was completed in January 1986. All 88 Skyhawks came from storage at Davis-Monthan, and comprised A-4Cs: 145064, 145131, 147673, 147675, 147696, 147722, 147726, 148500, 148502, 148509, 148573, 148575, 148576, 148593, 148597, 149547, 149550, 149575, 149580, 149581, 149595, 149606, 149636, 150581 and 150592 plus A-4Ls: 145065, 145076, 145078, 145092, 145101, 145103, 145114, 145119, 145121, 145128, 145141, 147669, 147671, 147690, 147703, 147706, 147736, 147754, 147761, 147768, 147780, 147782, 147793, 147796, 147798, 147802, 147807, 147815, 147827, 147836, 148306, 148307, 148316, 148436, 148446, 148479, 148555, 148581, 148588, 148602, 148611, 149497, 149500, 149502, 149506, 149518, 149531, 149536, 149540, 149551, 149555, 149573, 149583, 149591, 149594, 149604, 149607, 149608, 149620, 149626, 149630, 149633 and 150593.

A-4Q   16 A-4B aircraft modified for Argentine Navy.

A-4S   40 A-4B aircraft modified for Singaporean Air Force. Local serial numbers are 600-607, 616-622, 630-636, 643-650, 656-660 and 679-683. Previous identities, where known, are as follows: 600/142850, 601/142832, 602/142771, 603/142908, 604/142131, 605/144874, 606/144980, 607/145013, 616/142101, 619/142125, 621/142711, 630/142744, 631/142746, 632/142751, 633/142770, 634/142800, 636/142819, 643/142840, 645/142870, 646/142876, 647/142882, 650/142942, 656/144926, 659/144971, 660/144974, 679/145030, 680/145038, 681/145046, 682/145056, 683/145059.

TA-4S   7 A-4B aircraft modified for Singaporean Air Force. Local serial numbers are 651-653 and 687-690. Previous identities, where known, are: 651/145047, 653/145043 and 687/144894.

A-4S-1   70 A-4C and 16 A-4B supplied to Singapore for modification to this and TA-4S-1 standard in on-going programme which should result in delivery of about 50 aircraft. Local serial numbers include 914, 916, 924, 926-929, 936, 942, 945, 948, 955, 956, 964, 967, 970, 971 and 973. Aircraft obtained from storage at Davis-Monthan comprise TA-4Bs: 142140, 142713, 142768, 142778, 142854, 142860, 142881, 142891, 144885, 144904, 144916, 144922, 144944, 144961, 145021 and 145041 plus A-4Cs: 145063, 145068, 145071, 145073, 145106, 145108, 145110, 145118, 145132, 147731, 147742, 147743, 147745, 147752, 147779, 147783, 147785, 147786, 147792, 147797, 147809, 147821, 147823, 147835, 147838, 147841, 147845, 148304, 148311, 148439, 148449, 148458, 148462, 148464, 148465, 148469, 148482, 148483, 148493, 148497, 148504, 148513, 148521, 148525, 148526, 148528, 148529, 148534, 148541, 148548, 148552, 148558, 148591, 148598, 148603, 148605, 149492, 149493, 149498, 149520, 149522, 149530, 149537, 149544, 149587, 149588, 149614, 149617, 149628 149629.

TA-4S-1   See A-4S-1 entry for details of A-4 aircraft supplied to Singapore for modification to this standard. Should result in delivery of eight aircraft; local identities observed to date comprise: 900, 902, 904, 907, 909 and 917, although there appears to be some doubt about the latter example.

In addition, quite a few other Skyhawks were modified for special test functions. In most instances, only isolated aircraft were involved and these usually conformed to the Navy policy of redesignation to indicate the change of mission. Example of this are provided by the NA-4C (145062), NA-4E (148613/614), NA-4F (152101), YA-4F (150050), NTA-4F (152102) and NA-4M (155049).

APPENDIX IV: REGULAR FORCE NAVY ATTACK SQUADRONS - 1956-87

VA-12	A-4A/B/C/E	1957-71	
VA-15	A-4B/C	1965-69	
VA-22	A-4B/C/F	1960-71	
VA-23	A-4B/C/E/F	1960-70	
VA-34	A-4A/B/C	1956-69	
VA-36	A-4B/C	1958-70	
VA-43	A-4A/B/C/E, TA-4F/J	1959-73	(operated A-4A as VF-21 1958-59. Redesignated VF-43 in 6/73, still with A-4)
VA-44	A-4A/B/C/E/F, TA-4F	1958-70	
VA-45	A-4E, TA-4F/J	1966-85	(Redesignated as VF-45 2/85, still with A-4)
VA-46	A4B/C/E	1958-68	
VA-55	A-4B/C/E/F	1959-75	
VA-56	A-4A/B/C/E	1958-68	
VA-64	A-4B/C	1961-70	
VA-66	A-4A/B/C	1958-70	
VA-72	A-4A/B/C/E	1956-69	
VA-76	A-4B/C	1959-69	
VA-81	A-4B/C/E	1959-70	
VA-83	A-4A/B/C/E	1957-70	
VA-86	A-4A/B/C/E	1957-67	
VA-93	A-4A/B/C/E/F	1956-69	
VA-94	A-4B/C/E	1958-71	
VA-95	A-4B/C	1965-70	
VA-106	A-4B/C/E	1958-69	
VA-112	A-4A/B/C	1959-70	
VA-113	A-4A/B/C/F	1957-68	
VA-125	A-4A/B/C/E/F, TA-4F	1958-ca71	
VA-126	A-4A/B/C	1959-61	
VA-127	A-4F, TA-4F/J	1966-date	
VA-133	A-4B	1961-62	
VA-134	A-4B	1961-62	
VA-144	A-4C/E/F	1962-70	
VA-146	A-4B/C	1962-68	
VA-152	A-4B/E	1968-71	
VA-153	A-4A/B/C/E/F	1957-69	
VA-155	A-4B/E/F	1958-69	
VA-163	A-4B/E	1960-69	
VA-164	A-4B/E/F	1960-75	
VA-172	A-4A/B/C	1957-71	
VA-192	A-4B/C/E/F	1959-70	
VA-195	A-4B/C/E	1959-70	
VA-212	A-4B/E/F	1961-75	
VA-216	A-4B/C/E	1962-70	

REGULAR FORCE NAVY ANTI-SUBMARINE FIGHTER SQUADRONS

VSF-1	A-4B/C	1965-70
VSF-3	A-4C	1967-68

REGULAR FORCE MARINE CORPS ATTACK SQUADRONS

VMA-121	A-4B/C/E	1958-69
VMA-211	A-4A/B/C/E/M	1957-date
VMA-212	A-4B	1961-63
VMA-214	A-4B/C/E/F/M	1961-date
VMA-223	A-4C/E/F/M	1961-date
VMA-224	A-4A/B/C/E	1956-66
VMA-225	A-4B/C	1958-66
VMA-242	A-4B/C	1960-64
VMA-311	A-4B/C/E/M	1958-date
VMA-324	A-4B/C/E/M	1959-74
VMA-331	A-4B/E/M	1959-83
VMA-332	A-4B/C/E	1958-68
VMA-533	A-4B/C	1959-65

Note: VMA-343 was due to convert from FJ-4 Fury to A-4 Skyhawk in 1961 but was probably disestablished before this took effect.